# Disclaimer

The information included in this book is desig[n]... information on the subjects discussed. This [book is] not meant to be used to diagnose or treat any medical condition. For diagnosis or treatment of any medical problem, consult your own doctor. The author and publisher are not responsible for any specific health or allergy needs that may require medical supervision and are not liable for any damages or negative consequences from any application, action, treatment, or preparation, to anyone reading or following the information in this book. Links may change and any references included are provided for informational purposes only.

# Writing Great Music

## *Creating Magnificent Melodies For Your Song Lyrics*

By Susan Hollister
Copyright © 2021

# Table of Contents

## Dedication

This book is dedicated to all the creative souls who want to bring their great ideas, gifts and music into the world.

I would also like to extend an *Extra Special Thank You* to Phyllis Hopper. Your insights, knowledge and artistry have been wonderful additions to this book.

# Introduction

Congratulations, you have made a great decision by purchasing this book filled with the best ways to write magnificent music for your lyrics. Whether you're just getting started or you want to boost your songs to the next level, this book will give you what you need. Get excited, because you are about to discover the complete creative process for crafting great music.

In the following pages you will discover a great process for developing the musical side of your songwriting, from melody to harmony, chords, and beyond. It's easy, when you take the process step by step; this book will give you a detailed guide, showing exactly what you need to do in order to craft wonderful melodies that will enhance the message of your song's lyrics.

I've made it fun to nurture your musical writing voice while, at the same time, honing your craft. I've included a wide variety of ideas, skills, techniques and activities, each designed to sharpen your music-writing abilities. You will be able to put each idea or technique into practice as soon as it is discussed, applying it immediately to your own music writing. Also included are exercises that will allow you to isolate and practice specific creative skills; over time, they will help you become a master of your craft.

The process I am about to share with you will easily work with any genre of music. Although the rhythms and harmonic structures may change, to answer to the kind of music you are writing, your song's underlying framework will remain the same. In this book, you can take whatever raw creative desire has moved you and turn it into musical reality. If you want to approach songwriting as a way to make money, this book will prepare you to complete quality songs at a steady pace, without burning yourself out.

If you're new, just beginning to explore your capacity for creating music, this book will start you off right. The process outlined here is one many other great songwriters have followed. As you work your way through the book, you will be guided, step by step, the whole way. All you'll need to do is simply repeat this process each time you want to write another song, making minor tweaks as necessary, so that over time you will eventually develop a great process that works best for you.

Even if you are an experienced songwriter, there will be plenty of strategies you may have not tried yet, as well as a few musical tools you may not have thought to use. Any one of these just might be *the* key you need to unlock your greatest creative potential.

The songwriting process I reveal in this book has been specifically organized in a way that will help you easily discover your natural strengths as a songwriter. You will be guided through easy-to-follow segments that you can master, one by one. Before you know it, you will have an entire song written!

I've also included lots of great tips to help you avoid hitting a writing slump, but If you hit a dry spell, you'll know exactly how to get out of it as quickly as possible.

If you want to write both music *and* the lyrics for your song, you'll find the two processes share some similarities. At the same time, each task in the writing process calls for a specific *type* of writing skill, so I've chosen to separate the topic of writing music from the work of writing lyrics, placing them into two different – but complementary – books. When you are ready to write the lyrics to your music, I would highly suggest my companion book to this one entitled, "**Writing Great Lyrics**: Creating Incredible Lyrics For Your Songs." By me, Susan Hollister

This companion book will give you an easy-to-follow process that will carry you from forming initial ideas to crafting full-blown lyrics, a step at a time. You'll find the best methods for structuring your song lyrics. You'll also learn how to shape your phrases so that each part of the song fits together perfectly to form an organic whole.

Whatever your motivation for songwriting, this book will help you to supercharge your creative gifts. Now, let's take some action and get on with **Writing Some Magnificent Music** for your song.

# Chapter 1: How To Be At Your Creative Best

Before we dive into work, let's take a few minutes to dump some unnecessary baggage and prepare to be at our creative best. Here are my best ideas for preparing your creative self to flourish.

## The Four Foundations Of Creativity

The four pillars for a life of writing music – or any form of creative activity – are **gratitude**, **mindfulness**, physical **exercise,** and quality **sleep**. These are the keys to unlocking all your creative potential.

## Gratitude

Gratitude is your bedrock footing for living at your very best. It is also the number one preventative medicine against the negative, the critical, and the judgmental, in short: anything that would erect a roadblock against whatever you want to accomplish in your life. Choosing to be grateful is a simple but often overlooked practice that can work wonders in your life, as well as the lives of everyone you touch. I would encourage you to consciously train yourself in a daily practice of gratitude. What follows are a couple simple ways you can painlessly work this into your daily life.

## Exercise: Gratitude, Part 1

Start by taking 30 seconds, five times a day, to think of all the things you are truly grateful for. Anchor your moments of gratitude to everyday activities, and let them trigger this practice. For example, when I open the blinds in my house each morning, I take a moment to choose gratitude for each item that catches my eye outside the window.

## Exercise: Gratitude, Part 2

Another way to express gratitude is to choose to desire good for a specific person. Whenever someone comes to mind, call them by name and say, "I bless you today with happiness." When you wish other people sheer happiness in their life, their happiness will boomerang back onto you.

## Physical Exercise

Do you want to have an impact on the world around you. Keep your body's moving parts in good working order. It's as simple as that.

Your body was built for movement, so honor this need by including physical activity as part of your daily routine. It'll help you think more clearly, especially when you give yourself short activity breaks throughout the day.

Thirty minutes of moderate activity, broken into small pieces and interspersed throughout your day, will be enough. I'm asking you to go *just a little* beyond what you're used to doing. Push yourself just *a bit* beyond what's comfortable. Climb those stairs *a little* more energetically than usual and feel your chest expand to breathe more deeply. Bend over *a little* farther than usual (gently now, don't bounce!) to pick something up, and let yourself feel those muscles stretch.

Each day, give yourself <u>one brief activity</u> that will fire up your body, revving up your heart for just five to eight minutes, that's all. Select an activity that's at least tolerable, if not downright enjoyable.

## Sleep

Quality sleep is the key to everything. Depending on your age, your body will need six to eight hours of mostly uninterrupted sleep each night. It uses this time to send nutrients to repair and restore your physical systems and to let your mind process and organize the sensory input from the day.

You can help your body wind down for sleep at the end of the day by cutting out caffeine and sugar a few hours before bed. You will find it easier to fall asleep if you have a pre-bed routine you follow every night; your routine could be as simple as turning off lights, checking doors, and brushing your teeth. You will also sleep more soundly if you go to bed at about the same time each night. All of these things tell your mind and your body that it's time to get ready to sleep.

For more information on getting great sleep, I recommend the book, "Why We Sleep" by Matthew Walker.

## Mindfulness

Mindfulness is the skill of being fully present in the current moment, observing without judgment or criticism, and participating in the moment – or not – by conscious choice. The ability to focus on the present moment in time is a superpower many people overlook. Still, if you can be present, in your body, here and now, you will be able to sustain music-writing over a considerable period of time. Focusing on the here and now is another way to prevent judgmental, fearful thoughts from gaining a toehold.

If our brains are full of pain from the past, anxiety over the future, and digital overstimulation crammed into every waking moment in between, it's nearly impossible to focus on what's here and now. To counteract all of this, I urge you to set aside specific blocks of time to look in the face of both past pains and future fears, working through them to free yourself to be *all here*, right now. As for digital stimulation, I urge you to break your digital dependency by choosing to "fast" temporarily from phone, computer, radio, and television on a periodic basis. As you set boundaries around your greatest distractions, you will become much more mindful.

Living in the present won't come easily at first, yet if you can master this skill you won't regret it. It took me a long time to truly learn how to live in the moment, but the results have been absolutely amazing. It's made me happier and more productive, and I'm now actually living a much more enjoyable life.

Keep working at this. It will take time, but eventually you will find yourself easily resting in the present moment, fully alert, and able to perform at your very best throughout the day. That's mindfulness at its best.

For more information on how to live in the present moment, I recommend the book, "The Power of Now" by Eckhart Tolle.

Now that we've cleared the decks for action, let's get started on your next song!

# Chapter 2: Awaken Your Inner Musician

## What You Need To Know First

Because this is a book about songwriting and not a tutorial on developing performing skills or music theory, you need to already have a few basic skill essentials. You need to be able to figure out a melody and how to note down a basic rhythmic and chordal structure for your song. You need to be able to tell whether a pitch is going up or down, to be able to sing a pitch that you hear, and generally know how to follow music when you see it written on paper. I'll explain a lot as we go along, but for this book to be effective, you should already have a rough grasp of the basics already.

## Just Follow Along

I've designed this book to get you started with music writing and to keep you going strong over the long term. The focus of this book revolves around the process of creating music to complement a set of lyrics. It is *not* intended to be an end-all comprehensive description of music theory – such a description would take so long that it would fill many novels and you'd never get around to writing anything.

No, my objective is to give you a starter kit – the practical basics you'll need in order to get started writing music immediately. To start off with, you should already know the basics of reading music. Secondly, you'll benefit the most from this process if you apply what you're reading <u>to some actual lyrics</u>. Either write some of your own or "borrow" lyrics from a book of poetry or from an existing song.

Beginning with your chosen lyrics, you'll work through the exercises as they're presented, in order to develop your song. These exercises represent the various tools you will pick up in order to discover the music that best fits the words, mood, and message of your lyrics.

During the first few chapters, you can complete all the exercises without writing a lick of music, if necessary. By the time we start writing harmony, however, I will require you to write down actual notes. I will suggest some applications that can help you bridge the gap between singing your melody and writing it on the five-line staff, but the work of learning to read music is up to you. Fortunately, you'll have a few chapters in this book where no writing is required, so you can use that time to learn, on your own, how to notate melodies.

If you already read music, it won't take much to write down first the melodic line, and then the various harmonies as they are discussed. At the same time, I'll offer you some tools that can speed the process along and make it as pain-free as possible.

As you read this book, I suggest you:
- Actively participate – stop whenever I mention a song title and listen to the song. While you are listening ask yourself, "Why did she use this particular example?"

- Follow along – compose music to your own set of lyrics as we progress through the book.

- Repeat the process in this book over and over until it becomes a habit.

- Refer back to this book frequently, following the outlined processes and working through the exercises, as you continue to develop your music-writing skills.

Whether you're considering a professional career as a composer or arranger, or you're writing just for fun, I strongly recommend that you commit to writing at least five songs before you make up your mind to continue or quit. By the time you've worked through the process of setting five songs to music, you'll have a pretty good feel for how it works. You will also have overcome the biggest challenges and proven to yourself that you *can* persevere to the end, no matter what.

Keep in mind that music composition is a skill. You've only begun to touch the surface, let alone scratch it. You'll need to keep at it, over time, in order to explore the depths of your creative music writing potential.

Your skill will grow with each song you write. Once you've "finished" a song, even if you're not happy with the results (and some songs keep asking to be re-written; they'll never be *truly* finished), there's no need to consider the hours you spent wrestling it into submission as a waste of your time. Each hour you spend working on your craft is an hour invested, invested in honing your skills as you head toward expertise.

## You Know More Than You Think You Know

You know more about music than you might imagine. After all, you've been surrounded by it your entire life. From the birdsong outside your window to the music you listen to in your car, there are few places where music doesn't play a part in your life.

Getting married. You include music in both the ceremony and the celebration that follows. Working. What sort of background music helps you work at your best. Watching the game. Every lull in the action is punctuated by music. Relaxing. What kind of music helps you to de-stress and chill after a hard day or a tough week. Everywhere you go, music is in the backdrop of your life.

We may complain about background music, but it's there for a purpose. Just as subdued lighting sets the stage for an elegant romantic dinner at a high-class restaurant, music can prepare your heart to receive beauty in any form.

How often do you turn on the radio to draw your mind away from the emotions churning inside. If you're feeling sad, do you listen to songs that express the depth of your emotions. Or, do you try to elevate your mood by listening to "happy" music. You instinctively know which kind of music "feels" right for the moment.

You may not know the technical terms, but you certainly can tell a song you enjoy from one that grates on your nerves. You usually instinctively know when music sounds angry or when a love song is playing.

It would be easy for me to slip into musical jargon, but I'm going avoid using technical terms for their own sake. As a songwriter, you already know their *meaning*, because you've experienced them in the music. If it's truly necessary, I'll give you the technical terms, but my goal is always to help you connect with what you instinctively know as a songwriter.

In the chapters that follow, I'll point out examples of the strategies you'll be using by referring to tunes pretty much everybody knows. These simple melodies may sound trite, but if you pay attention, you'll find these same strategies appearing in most songs that are popular today. They function the same, no matter what genre you're exploring.

I encourage you to familiarize yourself with each strategy as it is presented. Take the time necessary to experiment; examine its every facet until you're comfortable working with it and you can easily identify when to apply it to your own music writing.

## Writing Essentials

The most straightforward way to record your musical ideas is with paper, pencil, and an eraser. Manuscript paper is still available for purchase in music stores; it's that five-lined staff, repeated for pages and pages. Old school for sure, but it's still the simplest way to set down ideas if you're out and about. The easiest way to get your hands on blank manuscript paper is to find a free template online and print it out.

I recommend writing with pencil instead of ink, unless you're making a final copy. Sharpen your pencil frequently or, better yet, use a mechanical pencil. And don't forget the eraser; you'll need more eraser than what comes perched atop your pencil. Plus, most erasers are so abrasive they'll eat through the paper; they also tend to add graphite streaks where you least want them. Better to buy a high-polymer eraser; it'll erase cleanly without damaging the printed lines on your manuscript paper.

If you don't read and write music, tools are readily available to help you. Of course, you'll eventually want to gain this skill, but for the first few chapters you can relax, at this point; any kind of audio recording device or app will work.

## Audio Recording

In addition to your cell phone, you'll find all sorts of sound recording apps online. The most popular at the moment are:

- Ardour
- Audacity
- WavePad
- Wavosaur

## Song Transcription Assistance

I view this as a stopgap measure, while you're in the process of building up the technical skills of writing music down. There's no substitute for knowing how to set down on manuscript paper the music you think up. You must become musically literate if you intend to write music. There's no shortcut; since you want to be a music writer, you absolutely *must* do the necessary work to become proficient at writing down music. However, while you're working on these skills, there's no reason you can't get some temporary help along the way.

If you can sing melodies basically in tune but find it too challenging to write them down yourself, don't give up yet. Tap into your innate resourcefulness. Seek out someone to help you; there are a number of options available to help you get your song written down.

- Online services – Google's "music transcription service", to name the most prominent. For a price, people will work with you to get your music written down.

- Transcription software - Record your song, then access an online application to transform the audio version into written music. If reading music is hard for you, be sure to get a musician to proofread the resulting score, because inevitably, the machine will misinterpret what it hears at times and you'll need to do at least a little cleanup and correction.

- University students – Music majors will often be willing to help you get your song written out. Post your request on a student bulletin board or contact someone on the music faculty to ask for recommendations.

- Music studios/Music stores – these businesses will often have students who would benefit from the experience of helping you get your music written down. While most will do the work for free, at the same time, it would be only appropriate to offer them something for their services.

- Church musicians – Pianists, organists and other musicians associated with churches or synagogues will often be willing to help, if you ask politely, especially if you offer to give them something in exchange for their time and labor.

## What You Need To Know To Get Started

You will want to have a passing familiarity with the piano keyboard. It doesn't matter whether you're looking at a regular piano or an electronic keyboard; those white and black keys are what we'll use, whenever it's necessary to illustrate specific notes, chords, etc. If you play guitar or another instrument, you should know how to match what you're playing to a specific note on the musical staff. These skills will be sufficient for now.

You should also have a general understanding of how harmonies are structured to support your song's melody, but don't worry too much about this right now. You probably have an instinctive understanding of harmony, knowing where the chords belong and where they don't quite fit, so I'll avoid burdening you with too much complexity and just stick to the basics. When we start working with writing harmony, I'll provide a refresher course on the fundamentals as we go along.

There are plenty of resources available, both online and in print, to help you fill in any gaps in your music skills. You can easily find online guides that will walk you step by step through the fine details of reading notes, for starters, and will progress until you have the skills to analyze the harmonic structure of pretty much any musical piece. Just google the key words as I use them and you'll find plenty of online assistance.

You should also have some way of hearing your song. It doesn't matter whether you sing, whistle, play the kazoo, the trumpet, or the piano; you need some way to get your melody out into the air, where it can be heard.

## Music-writing Apps

There are many ways you can preserve your song that extend beyond manuscript paper and using your phone to record a selfie video. Music-writing applications are wonderful for anyone who wants to write music for any purpose. You can use them to write down your songs; you can easily change them into a key that best suits your instrument. You can use these apps to write music and instantly hear what you have written. This rapid feedback will help you learn what works well; you'll immediately recognize what strategies *don't* work, simply by listening to what you've written. These applications can even help you begin to learn how to write music, if you've never done it before.

Unless your ear is phenomenally well-trained, you'll frequently think of melodies in your head that just don't sound that good when you play them back. That's why this software is so awesome;

you can experiment, put together a melody, and keep changing it until you get something that sounds good.

You're also training your "ear" – the part of your brain that "hears" the music you think. The more you write notes and play them back, the more your imagination will be trained to "think" music that "works" in real life. These music-writing apps can accelerate your progress.

In order of popularity, the primary applications used for music writing are:

- Musescore – far and away the most widely used program for quick and dirty music composition; it's robust and better yet, it's free. It syncs well with a host of other applications and its features are steadily expanding and being improved upon by programmers who are musicians and engravers, so they understand the details of music notation.

- Finale – the next-most popular songwriting and composing application has varying access levels that range from the completely free to a paid version with all the bells and whistles you could ever ask for. This app has the steepest learning curve, but engravers (the professionals who correct the finest details of music on the staff for printing houses) prefer it.

- Sibelius – Used by fewer people, but still well worth checking out. It produces a professional appearance similar to Finale, but it's a lot easier to work with.

- Dorico – This newcomer to the scene is gaining a positive reputation among composers, music teachers, musicians, and engravers. As with Finale, it provides multiple levels of access to the application, beginning with a free version that is limited to a two-line staff. I haven't worked with Dorico yet, but I've heard it's a lot easier to learn to use than Finale, so I'd recommend checking it out.

- ScoreCloud – If you prefer to work and store your stuff in the cloud, take a look at this one. It's a newer addition to the field of music composition programs. I've heard it's not as robust as Musescore and Finale, but it's still a sound application and may prove adequate for your current needs.

- Lilypond – Has been around a long time; it has limitations, but is perfectly fine if all you need is to jot down musical ideas.

## Your Lyrics – Written or Borrowed

You should also have a set of lyrics you want to set to music. If you've written them yourself, that's wonderful; if not, find some. You can google song lyrics and grab one you find interesting. I suggest you stick to pop or country songs, because they tend to be pretty straightforward; rap lyrics could be interesting, as long as the rhythm of the spoken words isn't too complicated. If you want to write the lyrics yourself, then I highly recommend the companion book to this one: Writing Great Lyrics: Creating Incredible Lyrics For Your Songs"

For the purposes of working through this book, your lyrics must include:

- At least two verses (It's okay if you have more, but the exercises will assume two)

- A chorus

- A bridge

Sometimes you'll get lucky when searching for lyrics and these sections will be labelled for you. If you're not so lucky, just read the lyrics and figure out for yourself which lines of text correspond to the verses, which words make up the chorus (the part repeated after each verse), and which lines make up the standout paragraph known as the bridge.

**The Verses** provide background information and move the song along. Each verse will have the same structure: it usually includes four lines, also known as phrases. Each line will have the same number of syllables, with only a few exceptions. The rhyme scheme will match across all verses. For example, usually, the first and third lines will rhyme, but sometimes the second and fourth lines will rhyme instead. At any rate, each verse will have two rhyming lines, but the specific vowel that is rhymed may differ from verse to verse. We'll spend several chapters working out these details, so don't let the nitty gritty bother you at this point.

**The Chorus** is the _punch line_ of the song. Usually, four lines long with the same or a slightly different syllable length as the verse. The chorus is repeated immediately following each verse and it will usually be the last words the listener hears, at least for that song. You will use the chorus to focus the entire song upon a basic feeling. Your song title will usually appear within the chorus, as a full or partial phrase.

**The Bridge** is a contrasting section, different from both the verse and the chorus. It is only sung once, following the second verse and preceding the chorus. If the lyrics in the verses and the chorus are sedate, smooth and flowing, often the words in the bridge will be short, sharp, choppy and driving, just for contrast.

The bridge is where the song takes a sharp left turn (or right turn, or U-turn). This is where you surprise the listener with information that turns the perspective upside down or sheds new light on the situation. The bridge is usually four lines long, although even this may vary; the length of each line may be shorter – or longer – than the lines in the verse and chorus, depending on what you need to best communicate your message.

I strongly suggest that when you borrow lyrics, you use songs you don't know; otherwise, your mind will compete with the original melody, adding confusion to the process of creating unique music.

Of course, once you've completed this book – and you have finished writing your song – you'll want to play a recording of the original musical setting, just to see what the songwriter did with it. You may be surprised at the strategies you discover.

Alright, now that you've chosen your words and have all the parts labelled, it's prep time. Before you write the first note, you must immerse yourself in every detail of your lyrics.

# Chapter 3: Crafting Lyrics That Work

Before you can begin to write the music for your song, you must become intimately acquainted with the words you'll be working with. If you crafted the lyrics yourself, you already have a head start in this respect. But either way, you'll benefit greatly from walking through the exercises in this chapter. They will help you now and in the future.

While I know it can be tempting to skip over the exercise or to just read them without doing them can be tempting, you are only hurting yourself if you do so. If you want to be the best songwriter you can be, then you need to put in the effort and work through each exercise as it comes up. This will dramatically increase your chances of seeing great success and fulfilling your songwriting dreams. All great performers know that to be truly great you need to first master the fundamentals. This means continuing to practice the fundamentals on a regular basis to keep your skills sharp!

This chapter will familiarize you with the big picture of your lyrics, as well as the inter-relationship between the phrases and sections of your song. A musician looks at words slightly differently than a lyricist does. With the musician, the music is the focus. The music should serve the lyrics well, supporting their rhythms and stress patterns.

I'll be walking you through a process most musicians use – often instinctively – as they weave music around words. This will help you shift your thinking into music-writing mode.

Both the words and the music are important, equally important. You can think of the words as the gem and the music as the setting that causes the gem to sparkle on the hand. In this chapter, we're going to walk through a series of exercises that will prepare you to write music that causes your lyrics to positively *gleam*.

In reality, a singer-songwriter often develops the words and music all together, in a massive jumble. Composers may already know the information they need to extract from the lyrics in order to create the appropriate music.

If you usually write both words and the music at the same time, you may find yourself blending parts of music composition into your lyrics crafting. A musical idea may suggest itself as part of a lyrical phrase. If the music keeps flowing along with your wordcraft, by all means let it flow. Jot down those musical ideas when they appear during your lyrics-writing sessions. While you're working through this music-focused book, however, you'll *learn faster* if you **isolate the music writing from your lyrics crafting**.

I've broken down the music-writing process into a series of discrete steps. You'll make the most consistent progress in your writing if you consciously follow these steps, in the order given, until they become a habit (Around 30 days of consistent repetition); then you'll automatically look for each of these items whenever you encounter new lyrics.

Now, let's shift our minds into music-writing mode.

## Exercise: Supercharging Your Lyrics

For this exercise, and the ones that follow, you'll want a hardcopy of your lyrics. Print out or hand-write the words, allowing plenty of space between each line, so you can mark it up and scribble down your ideas that may eventually become great music.

Later in this chapter, you'll also need either a sheet of manuscript paper, an audio recorder, your cell phone camera, or music-writing software – whatever format works best for you to store your melody. Trust me; I know from experience that melodies stored in the head have a tendency to erase themselves from your mind or to morph into something unrecognizable, especially the ones you're actively developing!

1. Now, pick up your lyrics and read them aloud from start to finish, just to acquaint (or re-acquaint) yourself with the song as a whole. Start reading the lyrics faster, then slower,

27

until you have found a speed that seems to best fit the words. Here's where you'll want to mark any words that interrupt the flow of the song. Put a small check mark above these words; you'll have a chance to review these again as we move through the process.

2. Now read the whole song again at what you consider to be an appropriate pace. Pay attention to the natural rise and fall of your voice as you read each phrase as part of the song.

3. Read it a third time and put a mark above the places where your speaking voice reaches a peak. You can shift around the peaks and low points, playing with different emphases until you're satisfied that your phrasing draws attention to the appropriate words and phrases as you progress through the song.

4. As you work at writing the music, you'll sometimes find words that just don't fit. They may interrupt the flow of your words because the language is more formal than the song as a whole. Sometimes an archaic phrase will draw too much attention from the message. Look for words that seem to interrupt the rhythm and flow of the phrase. Look for anything that distracts from the message of the song and mark it, for future reference.

5. Look for words that interrupt the stress pattern of your reading. For example: if the word "today" is located where the rhythm of the song demands you stress the first syllable instead of the second, you have a conflict between the song's meter and the English language. Whatever the case, if your gut tells you something is amiss, trust it. If you can't say *why* a word doesn't fit, it's not important. Mark the word and move on. Trust your gut. As you work with the music, you may choose later on to change it. Or not.

## Exercise: Word Importance

Now that you're familiar with the rhythmic ebb and flow of your song's lyrics, it's time to back up and discover the relative emotional weight of the individual words. When you were reading them, which words stuck out to you as most meaningful, the most important. These are the words we want to take note of in this exercise.

1. Start with the bridge; look for a single word, or a two- to three-word phrase within the bridge that is the most important to the effectiveness of the song. What packs the strongest emotional punch when you read it. If you were to remove those words, how would it impact the rest of the song. Once you've identified these key words, underline them in your text.

2. Then move on to the first verse and do the same thing, followed by verse two.

3. Finally, underline the most powerful word or phrase in the chorus.

## Exercise: Phrase Importance

Now it's time to evaluate the relative emotional weight of each phrase. Each line of your lyrics has an overall message or a point it's trying to communicate. Its meaning will wield a certain emotional influence. We want to measure the relative emotional impact for each line of your lyrics.

1. Start with the first verse. On a scale of one to five, mark each line of the verse with an emotional intensity level. If the phrase is mostly factual and has little emotional impact, you would label it a One. If the phrase sticks out from all the other phrases in the verse, with a strong emotional impact that will blow your listeners away – that would be a Five.

2. Make the same evaluation for

a. The second verse,
b. The chorus and
c. The bridge.

3. Now go back and make sure your levels are consistent across the entire song. Ensure that your Fives are true Fives and your Threes are on a similar medium level of intensity.

You'll use this information later, to match the intensity of your music to the intensity of the lyrics.

## What's the Meter?

If you wrote the lyrics to this song yourself, you should already know the meter you've used. However, if you aren't familiar with the term, a brief description will follow, before we get into the body of the exercise.

**Meter** is a count of the syllables that make up each phrase. For example:
- *"Three blind mice; three blind mice"* has six syllables.
- *"See how they run; see how they run."* has eight syllables.
- *"They all ran after the farmer's wife"* has nine syllables ("after" and "farmer" have two syllables each).
- *"Who cut off their tails with a carving knife"* has 10 syllables.
- *"Have you ever seen such a sight in your life"* has 11 syllables.
- *"As three blind mice?"* has four syllables.

We write the meter of a song as the total of each line's syllable count, separating each number with a period. For example: the meter of the above song is written as: 6.8.9.10.11.4, with 6 being the number of syllables in the first line, 8 the number in the second, etc.

A song's meter will help you understand what kind of song you're going to write, whether it's a waltz (groups of 3 beats) or a march (left-right, left-right, oom-pa, loom-pa). It will determine the length of your musical phrases. The variations in meter will hint at the melodic variations that will be needed as you develop the music.

## Exercise: Your Song's Meter

1.  Write the meter for the verses of your song, counting the number of syllables in each line.  The meter should be identical (or almost identical) for all verses.

2.  Write the meter for the chorus; it sometimes is different from the verses, but not always.

3.  Write the meter for the bridge.  The bridge's meter should be different from everything else.

Now that you're **properly armed** with the most important details and improvements to your lyrics, *let's start building some music!*

# Chapter 4: The Foundations of Great Music

Before we go any further, I need to make sure we're all on the same page. Now, if you're a musician who is acquainted with what they call "music theory", you may choose to pass over this chapter entirely. However, if you suspect there may be gaps in your foundational knowledge, you should read what follows. By my way of thinking, a little review can only help.

**Your Takeaway:** When we're finished with this chapter, you'll know how to start picking out melodies for your lyrics. You'll also have a rudimentary understanding of how musical scales work and what to do with a key signature.

**Materials required:**
- A recording of your song

- A piece of manuscript paper (or composition software, e.g., Musescore)

- A piano keyboard. If there's no piano handy, then find an online keyboard that will sound the notes when you tap on the keys. Otherwise, just print off a keyboard that includes at least 20 white keys.

We'll start with the basic elements of music and combine them to show how music is constructed, at least in Western cultures. This is a brief summary, so I'll move pretty fast, not stopping to detail the "whys" behind the facts.

Because I'm dumping a truckload of information on you all at once, you may feel overwhelmed at times. Whenever this happens, back off and do something else for a while. Don't try to absorb the entire chapter in one massive gulp.

We have specific names for the parts of music I'll be describing, but don't let the "technical terms" intimidate you. I'll be talking about things you already know deep in your bones; you just may not have yet found words to describe them. Maybe you've invented your own words for them; if so, simply consider the "technical terms" as synonyms to your own words.

At any rate, what I'm talking about will probably sound at least vaguely familiar, because it's part of the music you've been surrounded by for all of your life. As soon as you understand what I'm describing, you can attach to it the label I'm giving you. With these names, we then will have a common language to use as we explore how songs in general – and your song in particular – can be shaped into a piece of music.

If, at any point, what I'm saying *doesn't* make sense, I urge you to google the term I'm discussing and explore for yourself what it means. While understanding may dawn on you over time as you continue to work on developing your songs, these basics are truly essential to the craft of songwriting, so please don't neglect them forever.

As a songwriter, you'll need to know the basic components that combine to make music. This will prepare you to converse intelligently when you interact with other people.

## The Scale

We'll start with what is probably the most familiar musical term. If I ask you to sing a scale, you'll probably start la-la-la-ing without hesitation. You may have learned the do-re-mi-fa-sol-la-ti-do sequence in elementary school. It was made famous by the song, "Doe, a Deer" from "The Sound of Music."

This musical scale is part of our culture, so even if you say you can't sing, the idea of it lives in your head, to the point that anything different sounds "off" somehow. If you question this, listen to examples of "microtonal music"; the music of John Schneider or Tolgahan Çoğulu will illustrate this. When some of the notes sound slightly out of tune, it's because the music is played according to different rules than what you're used to.

You can think of the word "scale" in the context of climbing, or "scaling" a wall. The musical scale has its bottom note firmly set on the ground and each note represents a rung up the ladder, or a step up the wall, eight in all. Of course, if you go up a scale, you can also come back down, but in music theory, the initial idea is that of going *up* a scale (this will come in handy later).

do   re   mi   fa   sol   la   ti   do

*Solfege System, Written on the C Major Scale*

In case you're wondering, the do-re-mi sequence (also known as *solfège* – French, or *solfeggio* – Italian) was invented in the 1100s as a way of showing how the individual notes interact and influence each other. This comes in handy when your song is too high or too low for someone to sing. In that case, you'll move the whole piece up or down. This is an example of *transposition,* which I will explain fully later on.

## Note Names

A   B   C   D   E   F   G

*Names of Notes in Treble Clef*

You may also be familiar with the letter names that go with specific notes. They range in alphabetical order from A to G, making up seven notes of the scale. Yet, we think of a scale as *eight* notes. That's because a scale starts on a specific note and ends on the same note name, just eight notes (or an *octave*) above it.

For example, the most common scale begins on C and continues up through D, E, F and G; then the lettering sequence begins again. In this example, the next note is A, then B and you end on the final C.

From that vantage point you can look down to the bottom note, an octave below; lo and behold, there's another C.

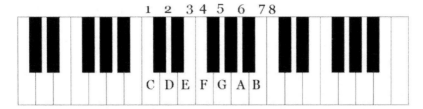

*C Major Scale with Note Names and Scale Step Numbers*

Are you wondering why we start on C instead of A. While the full explanation is too complex to detail here, you'll find some clues in the pages that describe *modes*. (Hint: visit ancient Greece.) For now, just accept that things start on C and wrap around to the next C otherwise people will hear something out of place. They may not be sure what… but they generally won't like it.

## Chromaticism

From here on out, I'll be sharing ideas that may not make sense to you at first, but trust me, they make musical sense even if the terminology doesn't. Nonetheless, go ahead and stuff it into your brain. It'll help you later.

The root word, "Chroma" means "color." There are 12 chromatic tones possible in our musical scale. We only play eight of them in any scale. What is *not* played is as important in determining the emotional color of a piece as the notes that *are* played. You'll understand this better as we go along.

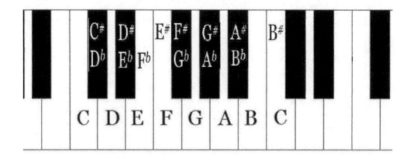

*Chromatic Tones with Their Alternate Note Names*

Black keys are what make it possible to transpose your song up or down and have it sound like the same melody. They show us where note names can be cut in half and where they can't. Even if this doesn't make sense to you, please bear with me as I go through the details. What *you learn here* will **prove vitally essential** to your songwriting.

What we've been working with since the start of this chapter is what we call a **major scale**. Since the overwhelming majority of popular songs in existence today are written using a major scale, we'll focus on that here. There will be time to mention exceptions to the rule later on.

## Exercise: The Shape of a Major Scale

Every major scale, regardless of the note it starts on, follows an identical sequence of half steps and whole steps between the notes. In this exercise, you're going to figure out the pattern for the major scale, using our old friend, the C scale.

Note: when I just use the letter to describe a scale or a chord, it stands for <u>a major scale</u> or chord. We say "minor" (or the lower case, "m") when a chord or a scale is minor. When I said "the C scale" above, I meant that it was a major scale. If I were talking about the minor scale, I would have said, "the C minor scale."

For this exercise, you'll need to look at your keyboard. Start by locating the note C. To find C, find a grouping of two black keys, touch the left black key, then land on the white key immediately to its left. We call that white note "C." Mark it so you can find it easily.

If you want, you can find and mark every C on the keyboard. This will make it easier to identify the surrounding notes, if you aren't necessarily comfortable moving about on a musical keyboard.

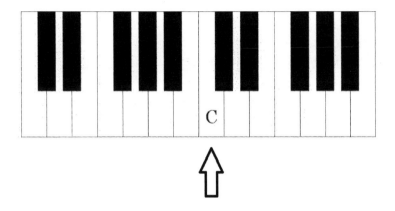

*Middle C on the Keyboard*

If you're working with a "real" piano, you can mark the C notes with blue painters' tape. To make your playing time more fun, you can mark your notes with a tiny shell, a gem, a small stone, a small sticky note, or anything you want. Just don't use anything so thin that it could fall through the cracks between the keys.

Fill in the following list with the number of half steps between each note. A half step is the distance between a key and the very next one, whether the next one is a white key or a black one. I've filled in a couple for you.

You'll notice that between C and D there are two half steps: one from C to C-sharp and the second from C-sharp to D. By contrast, the distance between E and F is a single half step, because there is no black key between the two notes. Now, go ahead and write how many half steps are found between the rest of the note pairs.

C to D:     **2**
D to E:

37

| | |
|---|---|
| E to F: | **1** |
| F to G: | |
| G to A: | |
| A to B: | |
| B to C: | |

Review the pattern you just filled in.  Notice that there are <u>only two places</u> where only a single half step appears: between scale steps **three and four** (E to F) and steps **seven and eight** (B to C).

Everything else is separated by *two* half steps; since two halves equal one whole, we say they have a <u>whole</u> step between them.  This is the pattern for every major scale.  You can start on any note and if you follow this pattern of putting a whole step (two half steps=2 piano keys) between each note except for steps 3 and 4, and 7 and 8,  then it will always sound like a major scale.

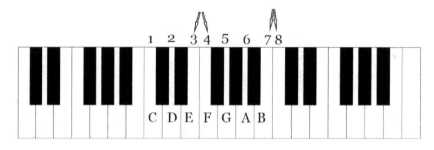

*C Major Scale, Showing Half Steps*

## Exercise: White Keys Only

For this exercise you'll want a piano or something more playable than a paper printout.  You'll want something you can actually hear.  If there's no real piano available, google "virtual piano" and you'll find several sites where you can play notes and hear what they sound like.  For example, as of this writing, www.pianu.com and www.virtualpiano.net allow you to play individual notes, using mouse clicks.

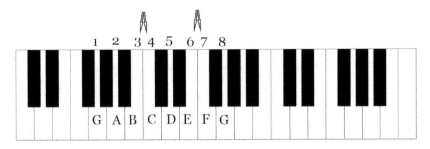

*G Scale on White Keys, with Half Steps Marked*

Using only white keys and starting on a G note, walk up the scale to the next G. Near the top, if you pay close attention, you'll hear something that sounds "off."

Let's look for the half steps. Find steps three and four; you'll notice there's no key between these two notes, so they make up the distance of a half step, which is correct for a major scale.

Now count the number of half steps between scale steps seven and eight. Did you count two half steps. That's the problem. There's supposed to be only a single half step between scale steps seven and eight. Hmmm.

Where'd the half step go. Which notes on the white keys are separated by a half step. If you answered B to C, you are correct; they have half step between them Where's the other half step on the white keys?

If you answered "between E and F" you are also correct. And there's the problem. There should be **two** half steps between the 6th and 7th notes of the scale but there's only one between E and F. To fix the problem, raise the F up by half a step. Whenever you raise a note like this, the black note gets the name of the key that was raised (in this case, F) followed by a sharp sign (#).

Now the final scale step matches the major scale pattern: F sharp (F#) is the 7th note of the scale and how it's just a half-step below G, the 8th step of the scale.

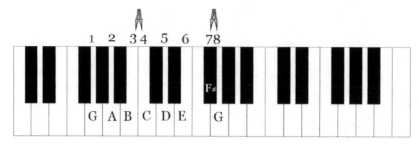

*G Major Scale*

## Practical Key Signatures

If you wanted to, you could perform this half-step-counting exercise to fill out the scales for each of the notes – A through G...and then for each of the black notes, too. However, this level of tedium is unnecessary because each of these keys has its own **"key signature"** so you'll know from the start of your song which notes are raised or lowered to fit into the pattern of its major scale.

The key signature is the clump of sharp signs (#) or flat signs (b) you see on the left side of a page of music. Remember: if there are *no* flat or sharp symbols in your key signature, it means the song is in the key of C; that means everything is played on the white keys.

## Reference: Key Signatures

For your reference, here are the key signatures you'll be most likely to use:

| Key | Key Signature |
|-----|---------------|
| C | (none) |
| G | $F^{\#}$ |
| D | $F^{\#}$, $C^{\#}$ |
| A | $F^{\#}$, $C^{\#}$, $G^{\#}$ |
| E | $F^{\#}$, $C^{\#}$, $G^{\#}$, $D^{\#}$ |

*Key Signatures – Common Sharp Keys*

| Key | Key Signature |
|---|---|
| F | B$\flat$ |
| B$\flat$ | B$\flat$, E$\flat$ |
| E$\flat$ | B$\flat$, E$\flat$, A$\flat$ |
| A$\flat$ | B$\flat$, E$\flat$, A$\flat$, D$\flat$ |

*Key Signatures – Common Flat Keys*

Other keys exist, but I doubt you'll need them, so I've omitted them from the list. You can always learn about them on your own, if you're interested.

## Major to Minor

*Author's note: You won't need this information to write your first few songs, so feel free to just skim it over for now, but keep it in mind **as you'll need it later on**.*

Most of the Western World's popular songs are written in what we've been talking about so far: major keys. If you write Country and Western songs, you'll notice that sad songs are often written in a minor key, where the third note in the scale is lowered a half step. The most common keys for sad Country songs are A minor (no sharps or flats) and E minor (only one sharp).

*A Minor Scale, E Minor Scale*

You probably can instinctively "hear" the sound of a minor song. The Beatles "Eleanor Rigby" provides an excellent example; their "Hey Jude", in contrast, is firmly in a major key. The Christmas Carol "We Three Kings" is a hybrid. The verses are in minor, but the chorus ("Star of wonder...") is in the *relative major* key (see below for a description).

## White Keys Only

If you experiment, you can find some interesting scale patterns by starting your scale on a different white key and playing an octave scale on only the white keys. These are what are called **modes**, but we won't go into them here, except to point out that the white-key scale pattern that starts on the note A, is what we call a minor scale; it's in a minor key, or a minor mode. Each major key is paired with what is called its **relative minor.** This is the minor key that has shares its key signature (the same number of flats or sharps) with what we call its "relative major" key.

Before you get too confused, all you need to remember is that a minor key uses the key signature of the major key that starts on its third scale step. For example. The key of A minor has the key signature that belongs with C major (the third note up the A minor scale).

*The Key of A Minor Shares Notes with C Major.*

## Modes

If you're curious about other modes, here's a brief crash course.

Remember when I had you measure the half and whole steps between the notes on the C scale. That was how you learned about what we could call the Major, or Ionian, mode. You see, you could start on any note and play just the white keys and you would be playing in the mode associated with that note.

The minor mode, in its purest form, is called the "Aeolian mode." The original names for all these modes are Greek, since the modes were first codified in ancient Greece. Some of the modes are more major in their "feel" while others tend to feel minor.

We've already talked about major and minor; these modes appear so often that we rarely view them as modes. The major key, as I've mentioned, is so prevalent that we don't even need to use the word "major." Any key, is assumed to be a major key unless specifically informed otherwise. If I tell you a song is in "the key of A", you can safely assume that I mean "A major." If I mean to mention the *minor* key, I'll say "A minor."

Most of the other modes are no longer in common usage today, but they do appear every once in a while. Dorian is a minor mode beginning on D (play the white keys up the scale). It sounds minor because of its first three notes. "Scarborough Fair" and "A Horse with No Name" are excellent examples.

The only other mode that crops up semi-frequently is Mixolydian mode. It's what you got when I had you play the G scale on all white notes. Using white keys only, you will hear a regular major scale. However, when you reach the final two notes, it plays a trick on you with that F natural, making you wonder if it's *really* a major scale. Prime examples of songs in Mixolydian mode are "Ramblin' Man", "Sweet Home Alabama" and the Beatles' "Norwegian Wood."

That's enough about the modes for now. Although there's much more ground we could cover, to venture further at this point would take us wandering along a major tangent and you'd risk never finishing your song. If you're still curious though, feel free to explore these intriguing modes on your own. You'll find plenty of examples, tutorials, and detailed explanations online.

When it comes to your current song, I recommend you stick to a major key. There'll be plenty of time, after you've mastered the art and science of songwriting, to explore the complex world of other modes. Eventually, your expanding musical preferences may push you to start developing songs that take you into the realm of modes beyond the Aeolian (major) and Ionian (minor).

## Minor Efforts

When you do choose to write in a minor mode, you'll need to figure out the key signature. We've already talked about how to go from a minor key to its relative major. Here's how to go the opposite direction, to take any *major* key and identify its *relative minor*. If you go down two scale steps from the key note of any major scale, you'll have the start of the relative minor scale. That scale is called "relative" because the two keys share the same key signature.

The simplest example is C major, since it has no sharps or flats in its key signature. If you go down from C two scale steps, you land on A. This means its relative minor is A. This works for any key. G's relative minor (down two scale steps: $F^\#$-E) is E minor, just to offer another example.

Here's a modified list of the keys and key signatures that I gave you earlier. I've expanded it to show you the relative minor keys associated with each key signature:

| Key | Key Signature | Relative Minor |
|---|---|---|
| C | (none) | A minor |
| G | $F^\#$ | E minor |
| D | $F^\#$, $C^\#$ | B minor |
| A | $F^\#$, $C^\#$, $G^\#$ | $F^\#$ minor |
| E | $F^\#$, $C^\#$, $G^\#$, $D^\#$ | $C^\#$ minor (very rarely used) |
| F | $B^b$ | D minor |
| $B^b$ | $B^b$, $E^b$ | G minor |
| $E^b$ | $B^b$, $E^b$, $A^b$ | C minor |
| $A^b$ | $B^b$, $E^b$, $A^b$, $D^b$ | F minor |

Now you know how to use minor keys in your writing. Keep in mind, however, that this is just a sparse overview of the minor mode. I highly recommend that you augment your musical experimentation with additional online information.

## Key Signature Notation

There's a beautiful mathematics to the way we think of music. It's based upon the physical properties of sound, so it makes sense that our notation should be governed by regular patterns.

When we draw in the flat symbols or the sharp symbols (never mixed; it's always all flats or all sharps) at the far-left edge of your first line of music, it "sets the tone" quite literally, for the entire piece. If your song shows both an F-sharp (F$^\#$) and a C-sharp (C$^\#$)marked at the beginning, it means that the rest of the song that unfolds before you will exist in a universe where the Fs and Cs are all elevated half a step – to F sharp and C sharp, respectively.

If there are two sharps in a piece, they are *always* F sharp and C sharp; written music is funny that way. If there are three sharps in a piece, you can add a G sharp sign after the F sharp and C sharp at the start of the piece. These are marked at the start of each line of music in the five-line staff.

The sharps are always added in this order: first comes F$^\#$, then down to C$^\#$, up to G$^\#$, down to D$^\#$, up to A$^\#$, down to E$^\#$ and finally, up to B$^\#$. Oddly enough, the flats always appear in the exact opposite order: first B$^\flat$, then up to E$^\flat$, followed by A$^\flat$, D$^\flat$, G$^\flat$, C$^\flat$ and F$^\flat$. They all have a standard location within the key signature, as represented below, in treble and bass clefs:

*Writing Sharps and Flats on the Staff*

Now that you know how music works and how to write it down, it's time to start developing a melody around your lyrics.

# Chapter 5: Having Fun With Melodies

This chapter will work your lyrics through a variety of melodic exercises. By the time you've completed them, you'll have the words down backwards, forwards, and sideways. In spite of the prolonged repetition, there is a method to my madness. Please stick with it through the entire process and you will see great results.

Each time you work through the lyrics, your understanding of them will deepen. The various exercises I've included will allow you to look at your words and their emerging melody from a variety of different angles.

Over time, as you continue to mull over words and melodies, you will begin to "see" both the big picture of the song – its overall message, the point it's trying to make – and the smaller arcs of melodic and poetic phrasing that contribute to the entire song. You'll see how each melodic phrase works to support and develop the song as a whole.

**Your Takeaways**:

1. A working melody for your song. It may be a rough draft, but at least you'll have something to start working from.

2. Strategies for absorbing the details in your lyrics that matter most to a musician.

3. A process for successfully developing a melody that best suits your lyrics.

If you're experienced in writing down music, go ahead and start writing down notes as soon as your melodic ideas emerge. This chapter is designed to accommodate writers who may not share your expertise, so feel free to substitute composing software for manuscript paper in any of the audio recording exercises that follow.

## Remain Flexible

We will begin by working through the lyrics, a phrase at a time, but as you progress through them, you'll be merging your melodic phrases together to add depth to the verses, enliven the chorus and empower the bridge, each of which will contribute to the overall shape and impact of your song. Please keep in mind that nowhere in this process are the words or the melody etched in stone. *Everything* – words, melody, phrasing, even meter – can be changed, thrown out and recreated, inverted, reversed, stretched, or compacted.

For this reason, it's essential that you remain flexible throughout this chapter and on throughout the rest of the book. Give yourself the freedom to grasp everything lightly, allowing it to grow into what it wants to be.

## Catching Patterns

Writing music is all about repeating and altering patterns and shapes. Once your eye and ear are trained, you'll notice patterns everywhere in the music. You'll see it in the harmonies and the rhythms, as well as in the melodic phrases of every song you hear and write.

*The First Phrase of "The Star-Spangled Banner"*

For example, the dramatic anthem, "The Star-Spangled Banner", starts with a melodic pattern that goes down for three notes, then rises for three notes, creating a V shape. That's the phrase, "Oh say, can you see." Then the pattern is repeated. Even though it starts on another pitch and the distance between each note is different, you have three notes down, followed by three notes up, another V-shaped pattern. Not only does the melody repeat its shape, so does the rhythm.

The next few notes, associated with the lyrics, "...proudly we hailed..." provide a new pattern, a stepwise descent down the scale. This is followed by an arpeggio that leaps down the current chord.

This entire pattern is repeated, note for note, to create the second musical phrase of the verse.

*The Second Half of "The Star-Spangled Banner"*

The third phrase is different, but the fourth returns to the inverse of the original shape: three-notes-*up* this time, followed by three-down. Then, in a grander scale, the entire melody so far repeats, creating a pattern made up of several smaller patterns. Then, as the song continues, different patterns emerge, have their day and subside, only to be replaced by new ones.

When you're writing your melody, pay attention to the patterns that emerge; consciously utilize them throughout your song. You'll be able to sense when a pattern has run its course and needs to be replaced by something else.

## Boredom vs. Disorientation

If your song starts to feel boring, this may be caused by repeating a pattern too many times. Your song can start to go round and round, digging a circular trench deeper and deeper and going nowhere fast. When this happens to your song, it's time to cut the melody loose and let it go flying off in a fresh direction. Back up to the previous phrase and start a new pattern. Or chuck the whole boring mess and start afresh.

Of course, the opposite extreme can also cause problems. Give it too much randomness and your song stops being a song and turns into an unrelated assemblage of notes. That's when you stop and _recall your original mission_: **to create a musical setting that will enhance the gem-like beauty of your lyrics**.

One way to avoid the extremes of boredom on one hand and randomness on the other is by the judicious use of musical motifs. I'm writing this in the melody chapter, but motifs include melodic, harmonic and rhythmic elements. Please keep this in mind as you read on.

## Questioning your Motifs

_Beethoven's 5th Symphony, opening motif_

A motif is a short musical idea that can is repeated in multiple spots throughout a song. The most famous motif of all time is probably the first four notes of Beethoven's Fifth Symphony. Almost everybody recognizes this, even if just by its rhythm alone: duh-duh-duh-duhhhh. To see how this motif can be used to tie a song together, give the piece a listen. The first minute of the piece is full of motif repetitions. While Beethoven's example is a little extreme, I hope you get the idea; a tastefully repeated motif can help to tie a song together.

*Start of Beethoven's 5th Symphony - Repetition of Opening Motif Highlighted*

If you have a snippet of melody that's exceptionally delightful, you can get away with repeating it in different places throughout the song. You can start it on a different note. You can repeat the rhythm, using entirely different notes in the melody. You can turn it upside down or you can even play it backwards. The possibilities for weaving a motif around your melody are almost endless. Even more opportunities will arise when we start talking about harmony.

Now, I don't recommend you saturate your song with a motif. It would actually become rather annoying, if not outright disruptive, to use a motif too frequently, even though Beethoven, in his genius, got away with it famously. No, a motif is best used as spice, sprinkled throughout your song. It can be used to emphasize a key word, to represent a specific characteristic, or to point out the song's title phrase. Use it selectively, where it fits.

There's no need to insist on using a motif. Don't fret if one resists your attempts to work it into different parts of your song. Some songs just refuse to work that way. However, if you find it useful, the use of motifs can add cohesiveness and depth to your work.

The best motifs fit so well – they're so subtly worked into the fabric of a song – that only an alert listener will pick up on them. However, that listener will give you high marks for your sly intelligence!

## Exercise: Johnny One Note

I'd like you to try a small experiment.  Begin by finding a place where you won't disturb anyone by singing out loud.  Your assignment is to sing "The Star-Spangled Banner." You're going to sing it with pathos, with enthusiasm, ***with all the emotion you can muster.***  The trick: you're only allowed to sing it on one pitch.  Go ahead; do it now!

So, how far did you get before you died of boredom.  As the early monks learned, you can say a lot by varying your volume and your intensity levels.  At the same time, you're seriously limited in the amount you can say musically when you're restricted to a single note.  When and how far you choose to move your melody up and down the scale is what makes it interesting.

## Use Your Full Range

We don't even *talk* in one pitch.  When we're surprised, thrilled, or angry, our pitch goes even higher than normal.  When you need to intimidate, when you're in the depths of your grief, or when the weight of your disappointment is too great to bear, your voice can descend to its lower limits.  If music is a way of expressing emotions, of communicating our most deeply-held values, then it makes sense that the most emotion-laden words we speak will carry the highest – or the very lowest – pitches.  The same holds true for our songs.

Take, for example, "The Star-Spangled Banner." The actual melody employs a broad melodic range and involves varying intensities in answer to the lyrics' full range of emotions.  If you read the lyrics, you'll note emotions that range from fear of defeat and anxious doubt, to glimmers of hope and then full-fledged rejoicing.  If you notice the melody, it starts up with a musical phrase that's repeated, as if the lyricist were pacing, worrying and wondering. These phrases state the question gnawing at the writer's heart.

The song continues in short puffs of revealing words, like the brief flashes of light that reveal, to the poet's eyes, the answer to his initial question. In the process, the melody wanders until the ending phrase. What we, today, hear as a triumphant, patriotic assertion is actually a question. Few people are aware that these lyrics are only the first stanza in a much longer poem. The question that ends the first verse, entices the reader onward, with additional questions that are never entirely answered until the final stanza of the song. (Be sure to look it up if you're curious.)

## Steps vs. Leaps

There are basically two ways a melody can move around. It can move up or down the scale note by note, or it can jump around. We'll revisit this subject in greater detail, but for now, here are the basic things you need to know.

An upward scale-wise (note-by-note) progression can build a sense of suspense or add tension. See the "Star-Spangled Banner" phrase, "O'er the land of the free" for a tension-building scale-wise phrase that demands a downward release (just try quitting the song there!)

When you move down the scale, it has the effect of releasing tension or of providing resolution and a fitting ending to a phrase or verse. Consider the ending phrase of the nursery rhyme, "Twinkle, Twinkle Little Star." The song ends with a downward scale on "how I wonder what you are."

When notes leap around, they can add or release tension by upward or downward movement. Huge leaps can grab your ears, from the start. Think of the verse of "Over the Rainbow" ("Somewhere..."), "Crazy" by Patsy Cline, or the start of the Oscar Meyer Wiener Song ("I wish...").

When songs use a series of leaps, it's often what we call an *arpeggio.* "The Star-Spangled Banner" opens with a downward and an upward arpeggio ("Oh, say, can you see"). Canada's national anthem opens with a scrambled arpeggio, but an arpeggio, nonetheless: "O, Canada." While we're on our tour of nations, France's national anthem, "La Marseillaise" is sprinkled with short arpeggios that travel in both directions. I suggest you try to pick them out as you listen to a recording. By sheer contrast, "God Save the Queen" is largely scale-wise in its motion. This gives it a very different feel from "La Marseillaise." It's interesting that both songs "feel" stately, but in different ways.

## Exercise: Melodies' Emotional Impact

Play a song from your playlist of all-time favorites. What emotions are expressed. Can you see how the melody adds to the emotional impact of the lyrics. What does the melody do to draw attention to important words or phrases. Does it move by steps, or by leaps. When the melody rises note by note, what happens to your emotions. What about when it slides down the scale?

If you can't see a vital emotional connection between the music and the lyrics after you've listened to the song several times, don't worry. Some melodies are more subtle than others. Simply, run through this exercise with another song. I suggest you listen to a song that has special meaning for you.

## Talk It Out

Now, it's time to return to your own lyrics. You may find it easier if you record yourself reading aloud, then listen to the recording according to the instructions below.

1. Try saying the first line of your first verse, as if you were in the middle of a conversation with a friend. Did you notice how your voice rose and fell. (Look for changes in pitch, volume, or intensity.)

2. Say it again and this time pay attention to the points where your voice rose, peaked and fell.

3. Review the lyrics of your first verse. How would you describe their mood. Are they cheerful. Bitter. Confused.

54

Put yourself in that mood. Then, speak the first verse, in that mood, like you would announce it to a roomful of people. Pay attention to which words were emphasized by slower or faster articulation, greater intensity, a higher pitch, or louder volume.

4.  Now, check back to your notes from the previous chapter. Look at where you marked the most important words in each line. Do the high points or the low points in your speaking voice match the key words in your phrases.

5.  If there are differences, check them out and trust your judgment to help you decide on the most effective way of putting forth the words. It may be more effective to change your lyrics around to better match the emphasis in your speaking. However, in some cases you may find your message is better served by shifting the spoken emphasis. Speak the verses, attempting to blend the best of your natural speech with the line-by-line emphasis you marked out earlier.

6.  When you're satisfied – at least for now – with the phrasing of your verses, draw a line above the words, representing where the pitch of your spoken voice should rise and where it should fall. Mark where the pitch could stay the same and where the change in pitch will be drastic.

Note that your meter must match in both verses. If you make a change to the meter of one, you will probably need to rework the other verse as well, until the meters of both verses match. Don't worry too intensely about meter, though. It is possible at times to cram two unstressed syllables into a single beat and get away with it or to stretch out a syllable to include more than one beat.

## Step-wise Movement

You make your melody interesting by repeating patterns, then by introducing new patterns, and then by altering them. The easiest pattern to follow is the scale-wise melody. A rising scale will *support increasing* <u>tension</u>, <u>anticipation</u>, <u>excitement</u> or <u>hope</u>. You can start your song on the beginning "key" note and sing up the scale as the arc of your phrase rises.

When the words are less important or as the excitement dies down, you can sing down the scale to release the tension, possibly ending the phrase on the bottom note of the scale. If you're not certain what I mean by "the bottom note", just sing your melody until it sounds "right."

You'll find an extreme example of a scale-wise melody in "Do (Doe) a Deer" from the classic musical, "The Sound of Music." Pretty much all you'll hear in this song is a scale-wise progression in the melody.

Beginning from "Sol" (Sew), the melody jumps down half an octave to the start of the scale, with "a needle... ." Then it travels up, scale-wise, until it just passes where it started. It then takes another leap back down, almost to the bottom, followed by another scale-wise rise and then continues the pattern until it's time to end the verse.

## Leaps, Take A Flying

Melodic jumps introduce variety into your melody. An exclusively scale-wise movement can become rather boring if not punctuated, at times, by interruptions. We'll talk more about the necessity of leaps between notes when we discuss what hides beneath your tune, namely the harmonic structure. For now, you can just think of melodic leaps as a way to infuse your song with interest.

Trust your instincts. Make the melodic leaps that sound right to you at this point and they'll probably be exactly what your song is needing.

The scale-wise nature of "Doe a Deer" is punctuated, especially in the second half, by melodic leaps. This provides a variety of stark contrast, even while it retains the comforting, predictable continuity of scale-wise movement.

## Tension, Delay and Release

What you're really doing through your melody is piling up tension to an almost unbearable point and then letting go of it. Repeatedly.

It's a fine line that you're walking. If you create too much tension without even a partial release to let off some of the pressure, your listeners will run away to get relief. Yet, if there's no tension at all (remember when you tried to sing the "Star Spangled Banner" on just one note?), your listeners will go to sleep or wander away, bored.

Your objective is to lead your audience with you on a magic journey. Like a fine storyteller, the path you describe is like life – sometimes smooth, sometimes rough or hilly, but always leading onward toward the journey's end. Along the way, you introduce elements into your melody that may surprise a listener, but the surprise will keep your audience engaged in the melodic story you are weaving.

Your listeners are trusting you to carry them onward toward a satisfactory conclusion. Yes, give them ups and downs, add to the mystery, build the tension, but don't forget to let them down gently in the end with a satisfying resolution, a pleasing, if not totally pleasant, ending.

The type of song you are writing will determine where and how much tension to build into your song and when you want to release it. In the Simon and Garfunkel classic, "Homeward Bound", the song begins with almost no tension, but it gradually builds, releasing only as the chorus winds down to prepare for the next verse. Some songs will be filled with tension, with themes involving pain, frustration and difficulty. However, even the darkest melodies have redemptive moments and they almost always provide a solid ending, even if not all the tensions are resolved.

## Creating Great Verses

Continue to develop your melody for the verses. Where the melody seems to belong, leave it as is, at least for now. Record your ideas, as you discover phrases you like, either in writing or by audio recording. In the parts you're not sure about, play around by heading off in different directions, melodically.

I suggest you experiment with these:

- Echo the melody of the previous phrase, starting on a different note.

- Introduce contrast. If the previous line of the song went downward, try moving the melody upward on this phrase and vice versa.

- Take a scale-wise melody and instead skip every other note on your way up or down.

- Try repeating a note across several syllables before moving the pitch up or down.

- Sing the phrase up the scale. Sing it down the scale. Then choose a direction and adjust the melody by putting small skips where it sounds like it needs it. Keep what sounds good.

- Vary the size of melodic jumps, adding greater leaps that end on words that are most important.

## Craft A Beautiful Chorus and An Excellent Bridge

You have two opportunities to build answering – or contrasting – melodies into the chorus and the bridge. These melodies should be different in rhythm and style from the verses and from each other. Yet, they must still fit within the song, as a whole.

## Writing the Chorus

The chorus is most closely tied to your verses. The end of a verse should be designed to feed directly into the chorus. This is an advantage, because you aren't starting from scratch; you are responding to the verse's melody.

You also want your chorus to end by leading the listener back to the next verse. The ending should be designed to mesh well with what will follow. Even though you'll be isolating the lyrics and melody of the chorus, you'll want to frequently check back with the verses to ensure that what you're writing allows you to move smoothly between the two.

Now, go ahead and delve into the chorus, the same way that you approached the verses:

1.  Speak aloud the lyrics of the <u>entire chorus</u>, just to refresh your memory.

2.  Review the melody in the <u>last line of the verses</u>, to give yourself a feel for where your chorus should start.

3.  Speak aloud the lyrics of the <u>first line</u> of your chorus. Use a conversational tone, shifting the stress, word lengths and the ups and downs of your voice in a way that best fits the lyrics. Jot down marks to indicate how your voice travelled across the first line

4.  Compare this <u>first phrase</u> (a.k.a., the first line) to the emphasis arc you drew earlier for these lyrics. If there are any differences between the two, decide which one you prefer to use and mark the inflections above the words.

5.  Now, work out a melody that generally follows the phrasing you marked out. This first pass doesn't have to be perfect, but give it your best shot. You'll have plenty of time at the end of this process to refine your ideas.

6.  Review the <u>first few notes of your verses</u> to remind yourself what will come after your chorus. Now, following the instructions in steps 3, 4 and 5 above, sketch out the verbal inflections and then form a melody for the **last line of your chorus.** Test your ending to make sure your song flows smoothly from the end of the chorus to the start of the next verse.

7.  Now, decide where <u>the peak of the chorus</u> should reside; put a mark above that location in the lyrics. Everything before that point will be building up to that peak, and your melody should release all the pent-up tension after that point.

8. Repeat steps 3, 4, and 5 for the <u>second line</u> of your chorus.

9. Repeat steps 3, 4, and 5 for the <u>third line</u> of your chorus.

10. Work with the chorus as a whole to mold a melody that contrasts with the verses, yet transitions smoothly to and from them. Remember to record your work so you don't lose it.

## Bridge Work

The bridge provides the greatest contrast to everything you've written so far. It should shake up the listeners, jar them awake enough to pay attention to both this "new" message and prepare them to view the final chorus from a fresh perspective.

The melody of both the chorus and the bridge should present a different "feel" from everything else. If a verse is smooth and softly undulating, the chorus will be more ear-catching if it is slightly choppy and angular in its sound. Then, when you reach the bridge, you can introduce a totally new feel.

If the melody of the verse has been softly swelling in its intensity, you'll want to match that intensity at the start of the chorus and add to it, letting the bridge pull out all the stops before returning it to the chorus for a strong ending.

Or not. Sometimes the contrast between the various sections can be sharp; other times you'll want to take a more subtle approach, changing the volume, melody and harmony slightly, but leaving the rhythm much the same. We'll talk about this more in the harmony and rhythm sections that follow. For now, just keep in mind that some sort of change needs to happen when you enter the bridge of your song.

## Creating A Masterful Bridge

You should be an expert in this process by now:

1. Talk through your bridge, using a conversational tone. Shift the stress, the length of words and the ups and downs of your voice.

2. Compare your results to the emphasis arcs you drew earlier for the bridge lyrics.

3. When you're comfortable with your phrasing, outline the arc of each line of the bridge.

4. Review the ending of the verses, so you have a feel for where to start your bridge melody. Sketch out a rough melody for the first line of the bridge.

5. Review the start of the chorus to remember what will be following your bridge. Then, sketch out a melody for the last line that will transition comfortably to the final chorus.

6. Now, mark your bridge's high point.

7. Develop a basic melody to match the shapes you outlined for the middle two lines.

8. Work with the bridge as a whole to build a melody that contrasts with the surrounding sections, but still transitions smoothly.

9. Remember to record, either via written notes, or in audio form, your entire song, including the bridge. As soon as you find something you're happy with, preserve it. You can always adjust it or replace it later on if you come up with a better idea.

**Great work.** With a solid draft of your melody recorded, we can start work on the supporting harmonic structure. Before we can do this however, you'll need a few music-writing skills, if you don't have them already. This is what we'll be tackling in the next chapter.

**Note**: if you already have your song written down, you can skip the chapter that follows and go directly into the next one.

# Chapter 6: Anchoring Your Melody

For many experienced musicians, the following exercises will be unnecessary, as you will have already settled on a key for your song and will have written down your melody. If so, you can skip this chapter and move on to the harmony-building phase.

For everyone else, especially if you are just beginning the process of writing down your own music, this chapter is tailored just for you.

**Your Takeaway:** The written melody to your entire song. It may not be perfect or polished, but it's something you can continue refining as you move forward to develop the harmonic structure.

## Magical Melodies

I've pushed this topic away, procrastinating as long as I can, but the day of reckoning has come. Up to now, you've been creating audio recordings of your melodic line. A lot of song development can be done audibly; it's *music* we're creating after all, and music is meant to be heard. However, at some point you'll need to pin down the specifics so other people can play along.

That point is now. It's time to learn the skill of putting down your melodies on paper.

You may have been able to put off learning how to write music for a long time. If you're *really* good at singing on key, you could probably sing your melody, even the harmony lines and then pay somebody to transcribe the music for you. Yet, you'll understand a lot better how music works if you actually write it out yourself.

## Old School

The basic way that most people start out is by using staff paper, also known as *manuscript paper.*

If you plan to use manuscript paper, here are a few guidelines to consider:

1. Keep a piece of professionally published music at hand and refer to it while you're writing. This will prove invaluable; it'll help you figure out the rules, such as where to write the clef sign and when you need to write down a key signature. It can even help with details like which side to put the stems of your notes and whether they should be pointing up or down.

2. Write in pencil and keep an eraser handy. You'll need more than just what is on the back end of your pencil; I'd recommend buying a high-polymer eraser because it will erase pencil marks cleanly without wearing through the paper or leaving pencil streaks.


3. Frequently stop and play back the music you've just written, to ensure you're still on track. I speak from my own experience; plenty of times I've started writing something in one key, then something distracts me and by the time I get back to writing, my mind is thinking in another key entirely. Frequent playbacks can catch the problem before it wanders too far astray!

## There's An App for That

Whether you're an expert or a beginner, I'd highly recommend you start using a music-writing application for most of your work. Yes, there's a learning curve with each one, but the sooner you start using one, the sooner you'll be comfortable with it. Even when you're first starting out, you'll discover you can save a heap of time and energy in the writing process by utilizing a music composition app.

Especially if you're just beginning to write down music, you can benefit hugely from the playback feature of these applications. You can actually hear each note as you enter it, making it less likely that your mind starts writing in another key. You can play back what you've written at any time, so you can audibly proofread and quickly correct anything that doesn't sound right.

## Exercise: Anchor Your Starting Note

Before you start working on harmonies, you must anchor your song in reality.  Until now, you've been just singing the melody however you want, not worrying about what the actual notes look like.  Now it's time to pick a good starting note.

The main reason to find a good starting note is practical: your song must be singable.  For example, have you ever started singing "The Star-Spangled Banner" only to discover you started so high that you can't reach "...the land of the free..." or so low that you run out of voice before you get all the way down to the "...twilight's last gleaming..."?

*The Melodic Range of "The Star-Spangled Banner"*

When you developed the melody for your song, you probably instinctively pitched it (started on a note that allowed you) to easily sing the whole thing.  You took into account how high and low the melody wandered and more or less started your song on a note that allowed you to sing it through comfortably.  If you got stuck, you only needed to start again, either higher or lower.

Now, all that's left is to locate – and name – your first note.  Sing your starting note, then use your instrument to discover the name for that note.  Go ahead; experiment until you have a letter name to put with that first note.

You may find your starting note is between two notes.  In that case, just adjust your voice up or down to start on a nearby pitch.

## Exercise: Find Your Key

Now that you have a starting note for your song, do you know what key you're singing in. A lot of times your starting note will be the bottom note of the scale, so you'll already know the key to your song.

Try this out: Try starting your song on C. Can you play your entire melody if you limit yourself to the white keys. If so, you're lucky; your starting note is the key of your song.

If that didn't work, don't lose heart. There are a few other strategies you can use to home in on the key. They consist of looking at:

- The last note of the song (in our case, the end of the chorus)
- The first downbeat (not always the first note)
- The gravitational point – The single note the song wants to gravitate toward.

## The Last Note

This is the strongest proof, although even this is not perfect. Consider the ending of "Twinkle, Twinkle Little Star." Here, the song ends precisely where it started. This song starts and ends on what we call the tonic (the bottom note of the scale). If your melody acts this way, you've now found your key.

Look at the end of "The Star-Spangled Banner" and "Mary Had a Little Lamb"; these all end on the tonic, or first note of the scale, although the songs do not start there. The former starts on the fifth, while "Mary..." starts with the third scale step.

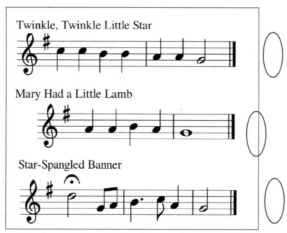

*Each song ends in the tonic note - G*

<u>What's the last note of your song.</u>  Is it identical to the melody's first note.  If so, there's a strong probability you've found your key.  However, don't take my word for it.  We have a couple more tests yet to run.

## First Downbeat

I say "downbeat" instead of "first note" because a lot of times a song will start with what we call a "pickup note" or an "upbeat".  These terms describe a song that begins on an unaccented beat or word, which could be any note at all, on or off the scale.

For example, "the Star-Spangled Banner" starts with two pickup notes (on the word, "Oh"); however, neither of them land on the bottom of the scale.  It's not until we reach the emphasized "Say" that we find the note that gives us our key.

*Song Beginnings, With Tonic Note Marked in Red*

The first <u>stressed</u> note in a song is usually either the first, third, or fifth note in the scale. That narrows down the possibilities, but it still isn't 100 percent foolproof. We're following a process of "triangulation", eliminating possibilities until we find the actual key.

<u>What note is on the first downbeat of your song.</u> Does it match the ending note. If so, you've probably found the key you're singing it in. To continue and verify this fact, let's try the next test. Even if you're not sure, hopefully this third test will clarify matters.

## Gravitational Point

The third point for triangulation is the gravitational point, or the **single note the entire song pulls toward**. If you quit singing "The Star-Spangled Banner" when you finished the words, "…O'er the ramparts we watched…" or after singing the phrase, "O'er the land of the free…," where does the song want to go. The note that ends both of these phrases is the song's gravitational point, it's the bottom-of-the-scale note.

Here's another way to find your song's gravitational center: listen to your melody and as you're listening, hum a note. See if you can hum a single note that will sound good through the entire song. Chances are, the note you're humming is *the tonic*, the first note of

67

the scale, and your song's key. In the remote chance that it isn't, you're probably humming either the 3$^{rd}$ or 5$^{th}$ of your scale.

Locate the note you're humming on a keyboard or other instrument. Does it match your song's ending. What about the first stressed note. Does all the evidence point toward a single note. If so, you've discovered the key for your song. **Congratulations.**

Note: If you're still unsure at this point, you will have already eliminated all but a few possibilities. Choose one of those possibilities and run with it for now. If you find later that you were wrong, it's a simple matter to adjust the key signature.

Now, all we need is your song's *starting* note!

## Exercise: Find The Tonic

This exercise is a wonderful way to train yourself to hear the key of any song. Here's the process:

1.  Any time you're listening to a song, start humming a single note that fits.

2.  Is your hummed note the same note the bass plays most of the time. Keep in mind that the bass note could be one or more octaves below your note, but it'll have the same note name. That common bass note is your key note, also known as the tonic.

3.  If you want to further verify that you've found the right note, locate that note on a piano or another instrument. Then google the song's chords to get the actual key. Keep in mind that people often change keys to better fit their own voices, but if you check an original recording with several lead sheets (chord sheets) for that song, the original key will probably be the most common one you find.

You can more easily verify your work if you know somebody who plays music on any instrument. Ask them to play a song while you listen. Hum what you think is the key note. Ask them to tell you if the note you are humming matches the key signature of the piece.

## Exercise: Make Your Key Playable

Now that you know what the key is for your song, this doesn't mean you must keep that key forever. That's the fun thing about music; your song can be moved around to any key you want.

Well, you can *sing* it in any key your voice can reach; some of those keys are pretty challenging to play on an instrument. I suggest you let this influence the key you write your music in. If you're writing for somebody else, go ahead and write in the key that is easiest for you; then, when you're done, change the key of the song to what the other person wants.

Guitars and most stringed instruments play music most easily when it's in sharp keys (keys with sharps in the key signature), but pianists tend to prefer to play flat keys. The cause for this preference lies in the way the instruments are structured.

For most pianists, the black notes are much easier to orient on and move around. However, most stringed instruments, have open strings that land on a piano's white keys. As a result, if you write your song in the key of A-flat (Ab), your pianist friend will be happy, but a guitar player or violinist won't be able to use any open strings when they play it. This won't trouble a professional-level player, but less accomplished musicians will find it a challenge to play.

Adjust your song's key, moving it around until it sounds right and will be easily playable by whatever instrument you're writing for. You can usually adjust the pitch up or down a note or two and still be able to sing the whole song.

It will work to your advantage if you can use a less complicated key signature. My advice: pick no more than two sharps or flats for your key signature.

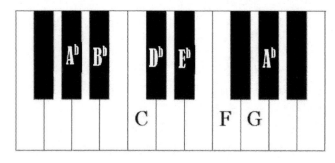

*A♭ Major Scale*

For example, if you find you're singing in A-flat (A♭ ), you'll be picking out your melody on almost no white keys. The key of A♭ has four flats, which is fine for advanced piano players, but not so easy for guitars, trombones, and other stringed instruments. If I were in your shoes, I'd move the key down by just a half step to G, which has only one sharp. However, if there's room to shift *up* a couple steps, you could comfortably sing your piece in C major, forgetting about flats or sharps altogether (hooray)!

At this point, select a key you can sing in that you can also easily write in. It's no big deal to change keys later on, especially if you're using music-writing software, so make life easy for yourself.

## Exercise: Prepare your Score

In order to write down your melody, you must decide on a few more things than the key of your song. If you're using a music-writing application like Musescore or Finale, the software will walk you through the process that you'll need to complete *before* you write the first note. However, if you're writing your melody on paper, here's the process to follow:

1.  Draw a treble clef sign at the start of the staff on your music paper.

2.  Choose a key for your song.

3. Determine your song's <u>key signature</u> (the number and names of the flats or sharps); then write it to the immediate right of the clef symbol.

4. Decide on the <u>time signature</u> of your piece. Does your melody have a duple beat (like a march) or a triple beat (like a waltz). If it has a duple beat, your time signature will probably be 4/4. If it's a waltz, it'll be 3/4 or 6/8. If you're unsure, choose the 4/4 time signature, just write it in pencil. If necessary, you can always change it, once you are certain.

   Note: write the time signature as two numerals, one above the other, without the slash that appeared in the previous paragraph.

5. Prepare a second and third staff in the same way, drawing in the treble clef sign, the time signature and then the key signature. You will use the second line for your simple harmony line in the next chapter, and the third line for entering in the chords, in the chapter after that.

6. Bind the three lines of staff together by drawing a vertical line down the left margin to connect the three staves ("staves" is the plural form of "staff"). Draw a similar line on the right margin.

7. Each time you start a new line of music, you'll prepare three staves and bind them together with a vertical line on each margin. Each staff will begin with:

   a. The clef sign and

   b. The key signature

   **Note**: <u>DO NOT</u> repeat the time signature at the start of each line of staff.

Key
Signature

Clef
Signs

Time
Signature

*Setting Up Your Score*

8.  Does your song start on a downbeat or an upbeat.  If it starts on an upbeat (an unstressed beat) you'll have a fraction of a measure to fill in with notes before you can draw the first barline; you'll write the stressed note that begins the first full measure of your melody immediately to the right of that barline.  Take "note" of the following examples:

*Pickup Notes*

## Exercise: Write An Amazing Melody

Your staff is now prepared, so it's time to start writing. Depending on how experienced you are at writing music, this process may take a few minutes to several hours. Feel free to spread out your writing across several days if necessary.

The following tips may prove helpful:

- First, write the notes of your first verse, spacing them a little apart; you'll be writing the lyrics beneath the notes.

- Keep all the note stems pointing up. When the stems are pointing up, they should be attached to the <u>right side</u> of the note head.

- If you're using manuscript paper, write in pencil.

- Frequently play back what you've written, to check for correctness.

When you've finished writing the music for the first verse, pencil in the lyrics:

- When writing the lyrics, put each syllable beneath the appropriate note.

- If a word is broken across two notes, separate the syllables by using a hyphen (a dash, "-") so you can see how the syllables and the words fit together with the music.

- Play through the entire first verse to proofread both the notes and the positioning of the lyrics. Make any necessary corrections.

- Compare the second verse to what you've already written; does the melody, as you've written it, work note for note with the lyrics of the second verse. If so, write the lyrics for the second verse beneath the lyrics for the first verse, matching syllable-by-syllable.

- If there are extra notes (e.g., pickup syllables) in the second verse, write these notes, with the stems pointing down, to indicate they are part of the second verse.

When you've finished the verses, repeat these same steps for writing the melody and lyrics to your chorus. Finally, write the bridge melody and its lyrics.

As we close out this chapter, step back and read the music you've written, singing the lyrics, to make sure that it's all correct. Does it sound okay. If anything doesn't sound quite right, take the time to **fix it right now**, before you move forward.

Next, we'll start figuring out some appropriate harmonies for your song. The easiest form of harmony is a simple line that flows along parallel to the melody. Harmony is a whole different ball game, so you'll want to come to the task refreshed and prepared to stretch your mind.  I suggest you give yourself a break before you tackle the next chapter.

# Chapter 7: Creating A Beautiful Harmonic Structure

Now that you have a melody sketched out, it's time to turn our attention toward its supporting harmonic structure.

Harmony is what you do when you sing along with the radio and find other notes to sing that sound just as good alongside the melody. If you play an instrument, harmony is when you find a bass line, a complementary second part, or chords that work well with the melody.

## Two Perspectives on Harmony

Harmony has both vertical and horizontal aspects. You can follow the shape of the melody, strengthening its progress over time by creating a complementary horizontal line of harmony. At the same time, the vertical aspect of harmony supports the song's solid harmonic foundation by stacking up support columns of notes atop notes, which we call chords. This chapter focuses on the horizontal aspects of harmony.

**The vertical element** of chords provides anchor points that move the song along what we call "the chord progression." Chords add depth of presence. They're what you find in backup vocals or rhythm guitar. This is the vertical element of harmony. In the chapter that follows this one, we'll get into the vertical chords that flesh out the harmonic structure and make it playable by a band or on a keyboard.

The **horizontal harmony** is like any romantic duet. While each solo voice may carry the melody alone at times, the other member of the duet will frequently chime in with a harmony line that agrees with and supports the melody. It's a form of agreement, like saying "u-huh" while you are listening to a friend tell you about their day.

**Your takeaway from this chapter:** a single harmony line to go with the melody of your song.

## Prerequisites

First, you'll need a written copy of your melody. I suggest you use the melody you developed in the previous chapter. If you have successfully followed those instructions, you should already have a copy of the melody line for your song, grouped with two empty staves beneath it. We will be filling in the first of those empty staves in this chapter.

If you don't have a written copy of your melody yet, go ahead and create one now, before you move forward. Include verses, chorus and bridge. You don't need to copy all the lyrics, but you'll want to include at least a key word or two at the start of each phrase, just to keep yourself oriented. And for each line of music you write, group together two more empty staves, for future use.

Secondly, you'll need an audio recording of your melody. You'll use this as you experiment with harmonies until they sound "right". Only after your harmony line sounds okay, will you commit it to paper. Of course, if you are using composing software, you'll be able to play back phrases as you write them, so you won't need to use the paper-and-pencil routine.

The easiest way to record the audio of your melody is to sing it into your phone. That way you can sing along with it and easily experiment with a variety of harmonies to find what sounds good and what best brings out the lyrics' message.

## Harmonic Tools

Most of this chapter consists of introducing you to the harmonic "tools" you'll be using. I'll describe what the basic forms of harmony look like and explain ways to apply them to your song's advantage.

Even if you're a songwriting expert, sometimes it helps to step back and take a look at the tools of your trade. You may even discover fresh uses for old harmonies.

Most writers tend to gravitate toward the same harmonic structures that are known and familiar. Over time, we can forget that other, equally valid, harmonic strategies exist. I'm hoping this review will help you rediscover a few of these harmonic strategies that you can use to great effect.

## Unison: All For One

This first tool is basic, but this makes it all the more valuable. I call it the "un-harmony", because you're doubling the same pitch as the melody.

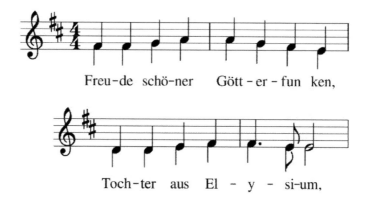

*From Beethoven's 9th Symphony, Unison Voices*

As simple as unison sounds, it can still be a powerful tool. When you need the ultimate in emphasis, simply add more voices or instruments on the melody and you'll get your point across more clearly. However, use this tool sparingly, or it will sound boring. IT CAN ALSO FEEL LIKE ALL CAPS SOUND IN YOUR HEAD – **LIKE CONSTANT SHOUTING.** Too much, and your audience will turn off the music just to get some peace and quiet.

The main point when writing harmony, is to provide variety. Unison should be employed strategically, to make a word or phrase stand out to the listener, but not to bludgeon them with a barrage of sound. Because melody notes will usually be the highest pitches, they will automatically stand out, so use unison reinforcement judiciously.

Unison can also have a **calming effect**. Listen to any Gregorian chant recording and you'll find your stresses washing away in the pure tones of masculine unison. You can use unison as an effective, ear-catching introduction, in sharp contrast to the rest of a melody that is full of rich harmonies.

If you want the effect of a **choir**, whether a group of children or a full-bodied adult choir, you can use unison in short bursts, to emphasize a phrase. Then move on to other forms of harmony.

## The Simple Octave

The octave is most often used with male-female duets, where it is easy to be mistaken for unison. It's easy to imagine that the male and female voices are singing identical pitches, but they're usually separated by an octave.

Freu-de schö-ner Gött-er-fun ken,

Toch-ter aus El - y - si-um,

*From Beethoven's 9th Symphony, Octave Voices*

Octave harmonizing is the easiest way to keep on singing the melody when it travels outside of your singing range. If the notes get too high, simply pop down an octave until you can reach them again, then pop back up again. In the same way, if the melody travels below your singing voice, simply jump up an octave until it's safe to return below to the original melody level.

Octave singing has an impact much like unison voices, yet with the broad open space between the two notes, the effect isn't quite as in-your-face as a unison passage would feel.  The octave is the most-used interval in choral arrangements; you'll often need it when you want both male and female voices to sing the melody.

## Shadowing: Thirds

The most common of the true harmonies, harmonies where you're actually singing a different note from the melody, is the third.  You start by going down two scale steps from the first melodic note.  This establishes a distance of a third from the melody.

You'll keep this distance as you shadow the melody.  When it moves up, you move up; when the pitch goes down, your harmony will fall as well, always keeping the same distance from the melody.

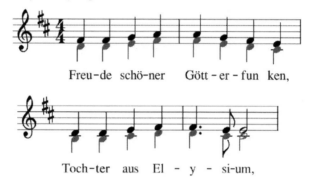

*From Beethoven's 9th Symphony, With Harmony Added a Third Below (in red)*

Sometimes a third just doesn't sound right.  You'll find that at times, the harmonic structure of a third below simply sounds wrong.  In this case, add another step down from the melody.  This will put the harmony a fourth below the melody, for just that note.  It'll usually be possible to return to a distance of a third for the next note, or the one after that.  You'll be able to hear what sounds good and adjust your harmony line to match it.

The reason for this adjustment is simple.  Your mind is already thinking of the whole three-note chord, even though you're only playing two of the notes.

In the following example, the second measure's final note now jumps down to the A below Middle C. It keeps that note for the first two syllables of the second line, then returns to shadowing the melody. This note is required by the supporting chord, which your mind knows, even though you may be consciously unaware of it. But don't spend time mulling over this mystery just yet. We'll unpack those details when we reach the next chapter and start fleshing out the rest of the chord.

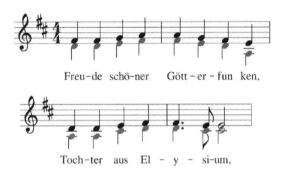

*From Beethoven's 9th Symphony, Modified Harmony a Third Below*

## Exercise: Unison, Octaves, Thirds

Now it's time to experiment with the harmonies we have discussed so far. **Note**: if you're able to write music at this point, go ahead and write down the notes once you know what they'll be; you can skip the recording process if you want. This process will be all the easier if you can use musical composition software, since you can use the playback feature to hear what works and what doesn't.

1. Leave the first two phrases from your <u>first verse</u> alone.

2. Record the rest of your first verse with yourself singing the melody in unison with yourself.

3. With the start of <u>Verse 2</u>, practice singing the first two lines an octave above or below the melody line. You can flip up or down if you need to in order to keep the octave within your singing range. When you're comfortable with octave singing, record yourself singing octaves for those two lines.

4. For the final two lines of the <u>second verse</u>, you'll be singing harmony a third (give or take a note or two) below the melody. Practice until you more-or-less know what you're doing, then record these two lines.

5. Listen to your recording. Describe briefly what each form of harmony does to its part of the song. Does it enhance the message in the lyrics. Detract from it?

6. Think about the whole piece, in light of the lyrics. Which portions would be most effective if sung in unison. Octaves. Thirds. Are there phrases that need to be emphasized by singing in unison. Where would a single voice be more effective. Are there places where the harmony of a third below would sound best?

7. Jot down your ideas on the lyrics sheet itself, above each line of lyrics.

## Flip the Third: Sixths

If harmonizing a third down becomes too repetitive, or if you want to introduce a voice that isn't low enough to handle a third below, you can flip this harmony up an octave. This makes it an interval of a perfect sixth *above* the melody. It's the exact same harmony notes as before, but because of the extra space between it and the melody, the music sounds less dense.

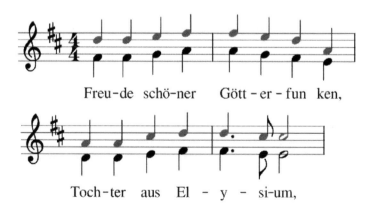

*From Beethoven's 9th Symphony, Harmony a Sixth Above (in red)*

## Exercise: Experiments In Harmony

Now, ignore your harmonizing ideas from the previous exercise:

1. Take a copy of your written melody for Verse One. Write in a harmony line that lies a third below it. (This is where composition software can come in handy; it allows you to experiment and hear instantly whether a harmony sounds "right" or not.)

2. Play the notes, both melody and harmony together, that you wrote. Are there places where the harmony just doesn't sound right.

3. In each space where the harmony just doesn't fit, lower the harmony note another step, or a half step. Play it to see if that solved the problem.

4. If the new harmony sounds fine, leave it. If your harmony still doesn't sound right, experiment. Try other nearby notes until you find a harmony that fits better. If you're still stumped, just erase the harmony from the troublesome note and move on for now.

You'll find that your instinct serves you well as you develop harmonic lines and build this structure of your song. Play each note with its harmony and keep working with it until the harmony line sounds good.

## Other Inversions

Each harmony note can be flipped up or down an octave, to create an interesting new sound. The third or sixth will get along more naturally with the melody than any other interval, but at times it sounds better to invert the other two intervals. You invert an interval by shifting either note down an octave, or up an octave.

2nd 7th        3rd 6th        4th 5th

*When the bottom note is flipped up an octave, it gives a more open sound.*

The closer your harmony line is to the melody, the more dissonant – or grating on the ear – it will sound. For example, if a harmony note is a second below the melody, you can flip the harmony up an octave and this will reduce the dissonance. However, don't bounce your harmony line around both below and on top of the melody. This will rarely provide a solution for a sustained melody line. Instead, keep your harmony on one side or the other of the melody

Often, an interval of a $2^{nd}$ will "resolve" (as it's called) the tension by lowering the bottom note to create a $3^{rd}$. Sometimes, it will sound right to lower the bottom note of a $4^{th}$ to resolve the sound to an open $5^{th}$. Your ear can usually tell you what sounds right.

## Counter-Melodies

The melody of a song is usually placed on the top line of musical notes. Because the highest pitch is most prominent, this area is usually reserved for the melodic line. If you hear in your mind a melodic line that lies consistently above the melody, you may be thinking of a **descant line**, also known as a counter-melody.

A counter-melody is an alternate melody that can run simultaneously with the first one. Sometimes it runs circles around the original melody as in the Bing Crosby tune, "Play a Simple Melody."

Other times, a counter-melody serves as both melody and harmony. Think of the round tune "Row, Row, Row Your Boat"; each part that enters the round is simultaneously a melody as well as a harmonic line that complements the melodies of the other three parts.

A counter-melody can add spice and sometimes extra lyrics, to a chorus, as you can hear in R.E.M.'s "Fall on Me." Your ear will also detect multiple counter-melodies, both vocal and instrumental, throughout "Truth Hurts" by Lizzo.

## Exercise: Review Harmony and Melody

"Señorita" by Shawn Mendes and Camila Cabello provides an artistic mix of every harmonic technique we've talked about so far. Listen to the song several times, identifying examples of:

- Unison

- Octave harmony

- Third harmony

- Descant

Let's use this song to also review the melodic traits we discussed back in Chapter 5. These melodic strategies may also be used as you develop your harmony line.

Listen again to "Señorita", searching both the harmonies and the melodic line for:

- Repeated notes,

- Scale-wise note movement up or down

- Scale-wise movement contrasted with arpeggios

- Scale-wise motion contrasted with leaps in pitch (e.g., "ooh-la-la-la")

- Melodic patterns that are repeated

- Melodic motifs that reappear throughout the song, possibly upside down and/or backwards

- Tension that builds and is sustained until a release point

## A Brief Description of Descant

This will be more important when your song is almost finished, but you need to know a bit for now.

Descant is the flavor of counter-melody that lives consistently *above* the melodic line. It serves as a second melody that doesn't clash with the original, but takes off on its own and simply *flies* above rest of the music. A most striking form of descant appears

85

in Souza's march, "The Stars and Stripes Forever", when the piccolo takes flight well above the melody.

Rhythmically, counter-melodies can provide a contrast to the more "straight" original melody. In the Crosby tune I mentioned above, the original melody strides forward steadily, beat for beat, but the counter-melody leaps, soars, dances and circles around the melody.

## Exercise: A Chorus Line

Now that you have a basic harmony to support your verses, it's time to develop a similar harmonic line for your chorus. Take your time to develop a horizontal harmony that sounds good when played with the melody.

Start by writing a harmony a third below the melody, then tweak the notes that don't work until they sound right.

## Exercise: Bridge Harmony Line

Take a minute and listen to your song so far. Hopefully, your verses and chorus sound like they belong to the same song, even if their melodic, rhythmic, and harmonic structure may vary.

Now, invent a harmony line for your bridge. Follow the same process we've been using, shadowing the melody a third or so below it. The harmonic line will give you hints of the vertical chordal structure you'll be developing, as we move on into the next chapter.

Once you're happy with your bridge harmony, check to ensure your harmony smoothly transitions between verse, bridge and chorus. Usually everything will work out well. In a few instances, however, you'll hear problems that can be resolved by making a couple of adjustments.

After you're happy with the harmony you've written for the entire song, copy it onto the second staff of the score you prepared in the previous chapter. You're going to need it as we move forward.

# Chapter 8: Crafting An Incredible Vertical Stack

The horizontal harmonic line you just developed provides hints of the harmonic structure of a song, but you'll need a **lead sheet** to tell other musicians the details of what they need in order to play the vertical (harmonic) underpinnings of your song. Whether you plan to fully write out an accompaniment or you intend to just provide the chords, your song isn't complete until you have written names for the vertical stack, the details of the song's harmonic structure.

Do you know your way around a keyboard or a guitar, mandolin, banjo, accordion, or any other chordable instrument. If so, you'll have a grasp on how to play chords beneath a melody. That's what we will be working on now: selecting and writing down the underlying chordal structure of your song.

**Takeaway**: a lead sheet you can hand off to the musicians in your group or to another arranger for the creation of a piano score or orchestration.

## What's A Lead Sheet?

In short, a lead sheet is a way to represent your song without writing out the notes. It shows the chord names, located above the lyrics at the point of the song when they appear. This allows other musicians, even if they don't know the precise melody, to accompany your song.

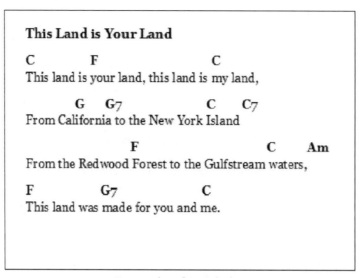

*Example of Lead Sheet*

If you know the melody, all you need in order to reproduce a song will be the chord names. However, to pass your song on to people who have yet to hear it, you'll need to write down the melody along with the lyrics and the chords.

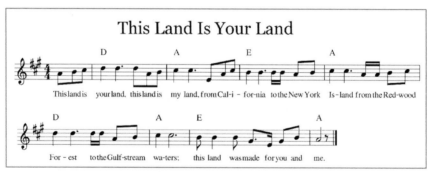

*Lead Sheet with Melody, Lyrics and Chords*

The good news is, once you've created this basic lead sheet, you can pass it on to a band or an arranger and these musicians will be able to flesh it out and bring your song to life before your very eyes.

## Necessary Tools

You'll need two things in order to complete the exercises in this chapter.

You'll want a **hardcopy** of the melody and harmony line you created in the previous chapter. This is the starting point for writing chord names as you work them out. You'll also want to include the lyrics, so you can immediately orient yourself within the song.

You will need **some way to play** the chords so you can hear them. If you're writing your music in an app like Musescore or Finale, you can easily play back anything you've written, tweaking your score until you're satisfied with it before you print out a final copy.

Barring that option, find a piano, an autoharp, anything that'll let you hear several notes played simultaneously. If that's not an option, you can still play chords one note at a time, but closely enough together that you get a sense of how the harmonic structure relates to both the melody and the other chords around it (in other words, you'll be playing *arpeggios*). Better yet, coerce a musical friend to help you. If your friend plays piano or guitar, all the better!

# This Land is Your Land

*Song Excerpt – Top staff: Block Chords,*
*Bottom staff: Chords as Arpeggios*

If all you have is your flute (or your trombone, or your violin), you *can* play the individual notes that make up a chord, if you turn them into arpeggios; it'll be harder to hear against the melody, but it can be done. Once you've figured out the chords, however, you'll still need to find someone who can play all the notes in block chords, along with your melody, just to be sure they work.

## Chord Notation – Introduction

**Note**: what follows is simply a brief survey of chord progressions. This is only a bare-bones kit to get you started. To become a skilled music writer, you'll want to move on from here to develop a much fuller understanding of musical harmony, chord progressions and harmonic structures.

The solfège system (do-re-mi…) helps us remember individual notes, the horizontal track, but we need a system for tracking the vertical chords as they change throughout your song. It's now time to introduce you to some basic chord progressions and to show you how to indicate their use.

Western music usually moves forward in a logical fashion. If you strip a song down to its most basic harmonies, you can accompany almost any song using only two or three different chords. All the other chords just add nuance, color (remember "chroma" from earlier?), and spice to your song.

## The Stack

All chords are, in their basic form, **triads** – groups of three notes plopped atop each other. For example, a C chord consists of the bottom note, C, along with the notes that are a third and a fifth above it. To find the third, start counting up the C scale: C is note 1, D is note 2 and E is note 3. So, the third note of the C chord is the note E.

To find the fifth above C, simply continue counting notes up the scale: F is 4 and G is 5. This means a C chord contains C, E and G in a vertical stack that is played simultaneously.

If you're wondering, they don't always appear stacked in this order; with a C, sometimes the E is on the bottom and other times the G can appear there instead of the C (see illustration, below). For example, look at the block chords in the earlier example. The final chord in the treble clef line is an A chord, but the third (the C-sharp) is written on the bottom of the stack. We call these **inversions,** but there's no need to focus on them right now. All you need to know for now is which chords to use and where to put them.

*C Triad, Showing Its Inversions*

## Tonic and Dominant

The two most essential chords in any song are built upon the first note and the fifth note of the scale. When we're working in C major, those notes – and their chords – are the C and the G (see the example below). These two chords are so important we've given them titles: the **tonic** for the first and the **dominant** for the fifth.

We use roman numerals to indicate where a chord lies on the current musical scale. The tonic is the first note of the scale for whatever key you are writing in. For example, if you're writing your song in the key of G, the first note of the scale, the tonic, will be G; G will be labelled with the roman numeral "I". If you're writing in F, the tonic note will be F and the roman numerals will follow up the scale, accordingly.

The tonic is given Roman numeral **I**; the dominant, built upon the fifth tone of the scale, is labelled **V**. As we wrote them before, the major chords use upper-case characters, while the minor chords are written in lower-case:

*Triads in the Key of C*

## Musical Tug-of-War

The tonic and the dominant in any key perform a balancing act together. These two chords are equal in power and act as opposite forces; think of them as positive and negative poles, as yin and yang, if you will. You can't have a song, or a song of any substance at any rate, without both of these fundamental forces coming into play.

The tonic is the foundation note.  It establishes your song's **key**. Everything else exists in relationship to this note.

The rest of the melody may travel all over the place, but the longer and further away it ventures from that tonic, the greater the tension is built up, demanding that it return "home" to the bottom line.

*The Gravitational Pull of the Tonic – "Twinkle, Twinkle Little Star"*

Practically speaking, the greatest musical tension appears when you play the dominant note and its associated chord.  The five chord in any key demands that you return home to the tonic.  The longer you delay this return, the more the suspense builds, up to a breaking point.  As you can see above, in this example, the melody begins on the tonic; it doesn't rest again until it closes out the phrase by returning to the tonic

There's a story told about the Bach household.  J. S. Bach had a huge family, all of whom were musical and rather mischievous. There's a well-known tale in which one member of the family in particular delighted in playing any composition until it landed on a *dominant* chord.  He would then walk away from the keyboard, leaving that dominant note lingering in the air, building up suspense, increasing the tension until somebody in the family couldn't stand it anymore and left whatever they were doing to rise, trek to the keyboard and strike the *tonic* chord, thereby **resolving** the tension.

Tension and resolution, the buildup and subsequent release, make up most of music.  Listen to any song; if you pay attention to the chords, you'll actually *feel* the tension building up in your body until it resolves at the tonic.

93

In this simple example, the middle phrase of "Twinkle, Twinkle Little Star" (the phrases, "up above..." and "Like a diamond...", illustrated below) basically plops down on a dominant chord and starts building tension. It begins on the dominant pitch (the V) and steps down the scale, almost touching the tonic but not quite. Then it teases you by jumping back up to the dominant note and scale-stepping down again, only resolving to the tonic chord when it begins the phrase that started the song.

*Example of melody traveling between the dominant (upper line) and the tonic (bottom line).*

## The Notation System

In the same way that the solfège system uses words to indicate the location of each melodic note, the harmonic notation system uses **roman numerals** to indicate where a melodic note is located within its key.

When you start stacking notes atop their base tone on the scale, you will notice something interesting. Some of the chords are major and some are minor. One is even a little weirder than that, but we won't worry about it for now.

## Exercise: Stacking Chords

List – **in pencil so you can change it** –the roman numerals from one (I) to seven (VII).

Now, start a second column. I want you to work in C major, so write "C" beside Roman numeral I, D beside Roman numeral II and so on, for each note of the C scale.

Using these note names, starting with the note C, write in the other two notes that make up the triad we call a C chord. Check your work against the notes we calculated in "The Stack" section above.

Now work down the list. For example, with the next note (D), you'll go up a third from D, using only white notes. Did you find F. Then travel up two more notes on the scale, which should give you an A.

Once you've completed your list, you should have a table that looks something like this:

| I | C | E | G |
|---|---|---|---|
| ii | D | F | A |
| iii | E | G | B |
| IV | F | A | C |
| V | G | B | D |
| vi | A | C | E |
| vii | B | D | F |

*Chords in the key of C major.*

## Exercise: Exploring Chords

I've shaded the tonic (I), the dominant (V) and the subdominant (IV). Listen to the notes of each of these chords as you play them. Now, play each of the remaining chords. What do the shaded chords have in common. What do the other chords have in common. Hint: check the intervals between the first two notes of each chord.

Were you able to find words to describe the difference. Yes, the I, IV and V chords are all major chords, while the rest are minor.

Minor chords are written in lower case Roman numerals. That's what I asked you to only pencil in the chord numbers. You can leave the shaded chord numbers in upper case, but I'd like you to rewrite the other roman numerals using lower case on your table, just as they appear in the above table.

## The Subdominant

While we've talked about the tonic (I) and how it is related to the dominant (V), we haven't yet discussed the other major chord, the one built upon the fourth scale step. We call this IV chord the **sub**dominant because of its pull toward the bottom scale tone is *almost* as powerful as the dominant's.

In church settings, it's the chord you hear when everyone sings "Amen" when a hymn is closing. The subdominant can also push toward the dominant chord, delaying resolution to the tonic. In the Beatles' "I Wanta Hold Your Hand"; the refrain consists of a IV-V-I progression.

## Those Other Chords

All the other chords that stack above the scale notes are minor. That is, the third of the chord is minor. The vii chord is weirder; not only is it minor, but the fifth of the chord is lowered, making it what we call a **diminished** chord. You'll be able to get along well without this for now, but put that on your list of details to learn about later. It's one of those chords that can add extra flavor and depth to your music.

For now, however, we'll stick to chords that form the basic foundation for your song.

## Basic Chord Progressions

It's said that you can play any song using only two (or at the most, three) chords. Those two chords are the tonic and dominant, along with – if necessary – the subdominant. That's why I had you calculate these three chords in the key of C. They can be calculated for the other keys later.

One of the games I made up when I was a child was to pick a specific note and mentally calculate the I, IV and V in that key. No, my childhood wasn't that boring; I just knew early on that I'd need to know this information, so I worked until I could calculate them quickly.

Here are a few of the most frequently used chord progressions:

**I – V – I:** The folk song, "Go Tell Aunt Rhody" matches perfectly. It has only two chords at its core:

> **I**                    **V**               **I**
> Go tell Aunt Rhody, go tell Aunt Rhody,
>
> **I**                         **V**                    **I**
> Go tell Aunt Rhody the old grey goose is dead.

*Two-chord Song, with Tonic (I) and Dominant (V) Marked*

**I – V – IV – I** (or I – IV – V – I): The hymn "Amazing Grace" has these chords as its base. Play the song that follows, substituting C for I, F for IV and G for V.

> **I**                              **IV**           **I**
> Amazing grace, how sweet the sound
>
>             **I**                          **V**
> That saved a wretch like me;
>
>           **I**                          **IV**        **I**
> I once was lost but now am found
>
>           **I**            **V**      **I**
> Was blind but now I see.

*Example of Chord Progression Using Tonic, Subdominant and Dominant Chords*

Now listen to a favorite song; see if you can pick out the tonic – the I – chord and the dominant (V) chord. Can you also hear when the subdominant (IV) is used?

Most blues songs are built on these three chords, with four or eight measures per chord. Listen to any blues song and you'll hear when the chords change, even if you don't know the name of the chord you're leaving and the new chord you're landing on!

**Pickup (V- I...)** – Sometimes a song won't start on the tonic note; sometimes it won't start even on the tonic chord. If so, the song will usually start on the dominant (V) which will usually appear in the form of a *pickup note*. See the starting notes of "Amazing Grace" above, which starts with a V-I progression, but the V is voiced *underneath* the rest of the melody instead of above it. The folk tune "Clementine" and the pop melody, "Perfect" both employ pickup notes, the former starting above the tonic and the latter starting below it. Contrast this with "Delicate", which has no pickup note.

## Exercise: Half Scales

While you can live without this skill, you'll have an easier time assigning chords to your songs when you memorize the note names that correspond to the tonic, subdominant and dominant chords for the keys you will use the most. Even if you haven't memorized them outright, you should at least learn to calculate them quickly, by counting up the scale.

For example, we'll use our basic <u>key of C</u>. Think "1, 2, 3, 4, 5" as you sing the note names up the scale: "C, D, E, F, G." Now sing the notes again, stressing the 1st, 4th and 5th notes on the scale: **1,** *2, 3,* **4, 5.** If you sing it correctly, the notes "C", "F" and "G" will come out the strongest.

You can do this for any key, in order to find the primary chords to use in your song. Do the same thing in the <u>key of G</u>. Sing the note names going up the G scale, stressing the 1st, 4th and 5th steps. Which notes were stressed. If you were successful, you should have discovered that the tonic, subdominant and dominant chords in the key of G are G, C and D.

Repeat this process for the first five notes of the <u>D scale</u>. **Hint**: in this key, the F is sharped (F#). What are the I, IV and V chords in the key of D. Check your answer below:

*I, IV and V chords in the key of D*

As you build up the chords above each scale step, keep in mind that in the key of D, where we're working now, the C is also sharped. The tonic chord, built upon the bottom note of the scale, consists of notes D, F-sharp and A. This time, G is the subdominant, while the dominant chord, A, is turned major by sharping the C. You can check it yourself by playing the notes and listening closely.

## Exercise: Practice Chord-Building

As a songwriter, you'll want to practice building chords until the process is completed easily. The faster you can build chords and visualize chord progressions, the easier it will be to transfer your musical ideas into writing without losing them in the process.

We've been reviewing major chords, since that's what your songs are built around: I, IV and V. Do you remember the special titles that belong to each of these chords. You can refresh your memory by looking back to the previous exercise.

To get started, write, one beneath the other, the roman numerals for:

- the dominant chord,
- the tonic, and
- the subdominant.

If you remembered these names correctly, you should now have a column that looks like this:

| V |
|---|
| I |
| IV |

The least complicated key to work with is C, so that's where we'll start. In the <u>key of C</u>, label each of these roman numerals with the appropriate note name. Your list should now look like:

| V | G |
|---|---|
| I | C |
| IV | F |

Now, write the notes for the rest of each chord, as they stack up in thirds. When you're finished you should have a table that looks somewhat like this:

| V | G | B | D |
|---|---|---|---|
| I | C | E | G |
| IV | F | A | C |

If you have enough musical experience, you may have found this exercise almost too easy. If the process was unfamiliar, however, I suggest you write out the tonic, subdominant, and dominant chords as soon as you know the key for a song you're writing. The more times you repeat this process, the easier it will become. Eventually, you'll be able to dispense with the table entirely, because it will already be in your head.

## Exercise: Duplicated Notes

Continue to use your results from the previous exercise.

Just for fun, there is one note that is the same in both the C and G chords; circle it. Now, circle the note that the F chord shares with the C chord. Does the F chord have any notes that match the G chord. Your results should look something like this:

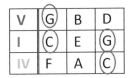

## Pick A Chord, Any Chord

So, how do you know which chord to use with a specific note in your melody. First, a few caveats:

1. <u>One chord can work for several notes.</u> Some notes are what we call "passing tones" because they are simply passing through the space between one chord and the next.

2. Almost always, <u>a new chord will land on an emphasized note,</u> that is, on the beat; very rarely will you change chords on an unstressed or off-beat note in the melody, at least not the simpler songs.

3. Almost every song can be simplified down to two or three chords: the tonic, the dominant and sometimes the subdominant as well. When you're writing your lead sheet, <u>focus on the placement of these chords first,</u> then fill in other chords only as needed, if they "make sense" – that is, if the song sounds incomplete without a different chord in that spot.

## Exercise: Chords in the Key of C

Now, starting halfway down a piece of paper, write each note in the C scale on a single line, leaving room between each note. Start with "C" and end with "C."

Begin your scale on C. **Write a roman numeral** "I" above this note, because we want to start on the tonic chord. Do the same with the last note on the scale.

Next, write IV and V above the F and G, respectively, drawing a box around both the chord name (the roman numeral) and note name for each one. Here is how your work will look:

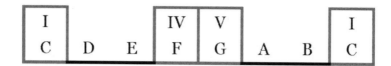

*C scale with Major chords marked.*

For the rest of the scale, take each note name and look for that note in the chord table you wrote out in the previous exercise. Write the correct Roman numeral for the chord that contains that note. If more than one will work, write them above each other, in any order.

When you're finished, you should have something that looks more-or-less like this:

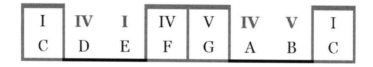

*C scale with all alternate chords marked.*

## How These Exercises Will Help You Write Music

At this point you may be wondering why I'm putting you through these brain-twisting exercises. Surely songwriters don't sit down and write tables like this before they put chords to their songs.

Well, no, but yes. Experienced songwriters have developed their chording skills over years of playing music and absorbing the formal music theory that lies behind it. They will have memorized each chord in a key, the key signatures, each chord's notes, and will understand how the chords interact with the notes that make up the melody. Through repeated use, these will all have been internalized, so your remembering and application are not automatic but organic. By organic, I mean that the response flows forth from your whole being easily and smoothly, not just from your logical, cognitive calculations.

However, until you can reach that point, you'll need to rely on these cognitive calculations and tools, a series of conscious decisions, and a methodical process. What I'm giving you is a crash course in the practical aspects of music theory, the stuff you'll need in order to build a harmonic structure for your song. I'm giving this to you piece by piece, in a step-by-step process you can repeat for each song you write. For now, just follow along; eventually, all the individual pieces will begin to work more smoothly together.

Over time, you'll internalize this practical understanding of how music works and these steps will become more-or-less automatic. But until that time, continue to train yourself by following these procedures.

How long, you may ask. Oh, only for about the first hundred songs or so. That may be an exaggeration, yet it's probably not too far off from the truth. The point is, these exercises are simply a means to an end. You are in the process of training your mind in the specific ways of thinking that are essential for writing music. You develop these mental skills just like you would learn the physical skills of running, jumping, driving a car, or baking a cake – by doing them. Over and over.

Your chording skills are only gained by repetition, *lots* of it. You'll need to repeat the process until it becomes second nature, and this may take a long time. So, make up your mind <u>now</u> that you're going to commit to doing whatever it takes to learn this skill!

## Exercise: Your Song's Chords

If you wrote your piece in C, you've already done all the work necessary, so just move on to the next exercise. If not, let's build the main chords for your song, as follows:

1. Start with three rows, the roman numerals IV, I and V:

| V | |
|---|---|
| I | |
| IV | |

2. Beside the roman numeral I in the middle row, write <u>your song's key</u>. If you sing your song in F, write "F" beside roman numeral I.

3. Sing up the scale, naming the notes as you go, until you reach the fifth scale step. (If you're in F, you would sing "F, G, A, B$^b$, C.") Write that fifth note name beside the roman numeral V; this is the first note in <u>your</u> dominant chord.

4. Go back down one scale step from the dominant and you have the subdominant; write this note beside roman numeral IV.

5. Now that you have the bottom notes of each of these chords, build the third and fifth of each chord. **Note:** you'll need to consult the key signature for your song, so you'll know which notes are sharped or flatted. For example, if you're working in F, you'll need to write B-flat (B$^b$) on the 4$^{th}$ scale step.

6. Armed with this information, start your second diagram. Write the scale notes that represent the key for your song, leaving plenty of space above the line for your chord names.

7. Locate the tonic, the subdominant, and the dominant notes in the scale and write the appropriate roman numeral above these notes (I, IV, V).

8. Draw a box surrounding the chord and the note name for these three chords. These are the notes that pretty much demand you play this particular chord when it appears.

9. For each remaining note in the scale, look for the chord (I, IV, or V) that has that note. When that note appears, you will probably need to play that particular chord.

## Bare-Bones Chording

Remember when I said that you can play almost any song using two, or at the most three, different chords. Let's try this on your song. Of course, other chords can add flavor and depth to your music and we'll get to that, but for now, you want to establish a basic framework. Let's begin by working on the bare essentials: the I and V chords in your song's key.

For the exercises that follow, you'll use the score you've already written for your song. Write in pencil, to more easily change things around, as needed.

You'll also need the tables you built in the previous exercise ("Your Song's Chords").

## Exercise: Great Verse Chords

Here's a simple process for building the chordal framework for your song. While it won't provide you the nuanced details, it will at least help you to develop the basic harmonic outline of your song.

1. Establish the key of your song, writing the names of each note in the tonic (I), the subdominant (IV) and the dominant (V) chords for this key. You'll be using these exclusively throughout this exercise.

2. Start by playing your song's I chord as you begin to sing your first verse. Go ahead and pencil in the note name of this chord (*not* the roman numeral) above the start of the melody line. Then play your song until the I chord doesn't sound right.

3. When the I chord sounds out of place, mark the name of the dominant (V) chord above your music and start playing it to your song. If something doesn't sound like it belongs, try playing the IV chord instead.

4. The music will want to return to the I chord at some point, so listen carefully for when your chord starts to sound out of place.

5. When this happens, switch back to the I chord, marking the note name of this chord above the melody note where you changed chords.

6. Continue this process, switching between the two chords as needed until you reach the end of the verse, which should finish either on the I chord or on the V chord, leading you into the chorus.

7. Sing the verse again, changing chords in the places you marked. Does everything sound right.

8. If the V chord prefers to wander off somewhere else before it returns to the tonic, try the IV chord.

9. If that doesn't fit, try the vi chord.

10. If you're still not satisfied, throw up your hands in let out a wail of utter despair. Just kidding. Don't do that. You already have a note from the harmony line that may help. Try building a triad using that harmony note, the melody note it goes with, and a third note on top or below. You may need to adjust the harmony note, too, if it still doesn't sound right

11. If still nothing works, just leave it without a chord and move on. All will be revealed in time, so have no worries.

12. Once you've assigned chords throughout this section of the song, go to the third staff. Mark this staff with a bass clef sign and write the bass notes that match the chord names you've already written.

13. Now, play the entire section, focusing on the melody and the block chords you just wrote out. If you hear anything that doesn't sound right, experiment with changes until you find something that works.

Sometimes, a single note will be the source of the problem. When this happens, either adjust the offending pitch or eliminate it altogether. Of course, you'll want to write down any changes you make as you go along.

## Exercise: Wonderful Chords For Your Chorus

Follow the above process with the chorus. Your chorus may begin with the subdominant or dominant chord, instead of the tonic. However, the chorus will usually end on the tonic (I) chord.

## Exercise: Powerful Bridge Chords

Follow the same process outlined above to create chords for the bridge section. Keep in mind that your melody may be very different in the bridge, so it may call for some variation in chords. You can try the ii chord instead of IV or the iii in place of the V chord, for example. Experiment until you find a chord that works.

Then write the letter name of the chord above the melody note where you start to use it.

## It's Just The Beginning

We've just begun to touch the surface of the intricate interplay between melodic and harmonic progression. You have the rest of your life to delve into the mysteries of **secondary dominants** (the V of V for example, where a chord begins on a fifth *above* the fifth note of the scale, but it's a Major chord), **seventh chords** (adding a major or a minor 7th above the base note of a chord, in addition to the rest of the triad), **augmented chords**, **diminished chords**...the list is endless. Yet, what you have figured out so far, is quite enough to get you started.

You'll find that you pick up ideas as you hear chords and work to figure out what they are and how they work with other chords. There are plenty of online tutorials available that can help you understand these concepts, and more. You've entered an amazing universe of sounds; I hope you enjoy exploring and learning more, applying it to your writing as you go.

## You Win!

<u>Congratulations.</u> You've completed your first song. Pat yourself on the back and give yourself a treat; you've earned it. Set aside your song, briefly. You want to gain enough perspective that when you return to it, you can listen with fresh ears.

When you return to your song, you may notice chords or harmonies that don't fit as smoothly as they did the last time you listened to it. This is normal. The song just needs a little more work. Continue to work with it and give your song the time it needs to settle into something you're happy with.

Once you've done this and are 100% happy with your song, you can create a beautiful arrangement for it yourself or hand your song off to a professional arranger who can take care of this for you.

# Chapter 9: The Path To Mastery

What's next. The second song, of course. Even if you aren't completely satisfied with your first song, it's time to set it aside and begin working on another song. After you've gained more experience in music writing, you discover, when you revisit this first song you'll immediately spot places where you can improve upon your earlier work. When this happens, *rejoice.* It's a sign that **your skills are growing.**

## Follow The Roadmap

You've completed the trip once, so the road should be more familiar the next time around. However, you can count on discovering contours in the musical landscape you may have never of noticed, each time you take the jaunt along this harmonic highway.

With each song, you'll encounter fresh challenges, so be ready to discover, learn, and get better. *It's a never-ending adventure.* If you do well, then over time, you can join the list of other great masters who have graced us with their brilliance on this planet.

*Do you have the courage to bring forth this work?*
*The treasures that are inside you are hoping you will say yes.*
*– Elizabeth Gilbert, in "Big Magic"*

On the surface, music writing can be a delightful, creative activity, calling out the best in your personality. When you're able to set words to music in a voice that sings true, there's no greater joy in life.

At the same time, composing music is hard work that can be exasperating at times. It will demand tons of time, the willingness to play a song over and over until you get it right and all the persistence you can muster. This book has been designed to help you spend your energies wisely, building a strong **foundational music writing practice** that is both *effective* and efficient. The process you've learned should enable you to set songs to beautiful music for many years to come.

I hope your journeys are blessed. Do your best to say something, musically, that goes beyond the trite, beyond the surface of life and that **delves deep into the very heart of how things truly are**. This is where all great songs reside.

# Chapter 10: How to Get Unstuck

Everybody gets stuck sometimes. Some people call it "writer's block", while others just call it a dry spell. This is all part of the rhythms of living. We have times when we're brimming with wonderful ideas; then there are those times when we feel lethargic and can't seem to come up with the motivation to proceed.

When things just aren't working right and when everything you try seems to bash you up against the same stone wall, it may be time to back off and try something else. What follows are some ideas I've used to generate fresh stamina and get the ball rolling again. I hope you'll refer to them any time you find yourself bogging down, growing weary, or just running out of ideas. Feel free to apply whatever appeals to you in the moment.

## Take A Diversion Break (Short Or Long).

Go back in this book to one of the exercises that appeals to you. Hopefully reworking one will help get you going again. Sometimes, just thinking about something else and taking action will be enough to give you a fresh perspective on what you're doing.

## Get Movin'

Jolt yourself out of your doldrums. Sometimes it helps to listen to music that is as different as possible from the kind of music you're working on. For this exercise, you don't even need words; simply find some music, crank up the speakers, stand up, and let the music move your body, even as it pours over you. Dance your little heart out!

## Work Through An Exercise That Targets Your Particular Problem.

There are plenty of exercises scattered throughout this book, each geared to help you sharpen your skills. Review them and choose one that addresses your current difficulty.

## Work A Crossword Puzzle

All right, crosswords may not be your thing. How about Sudoku. Solitaire. A board game. The idea is to do something that will fully occupy your brain and draw it away from the problem that has you bogged down. This will free up your subconscious to explore other possibilities while your conscious mind is otherwise occupied.

## Physical Distraction

Engage in any physical activity that demands a little mental concentration. If you're walking, pay attention to your breathing. Breathe in steadily until your lungs are full. Hold that fullness for a few paces, then exhale, taking twice as long to exhale as you took to inhale. Gradually add to how long you take to breathe in, continuing to double the length of your exhale. The act of coordinating your breathing with physical movement is enough to keep your mind off your writing for a few minutes.

## Not Quite Tai Chi

You can also practice walking, but in slow motion. Start out walking normally, then gradually slow your pace until you're consciously setting down your heel before lowering the rest of the sole, feeling the ground underneath your foot as you shift your weight, gradually and smoothly, onto the new foot.

When your weight is fully shifted onto the new foot, lift the other one, heel first and then toes, bending your knee to raise your leg in an exaggerated motion as you swing your leg forward to repeat the same process with the other foot.

The slower you can walk and still shift smoothly from one foot to the other will reveal how well you've developed your sense of balance. Over several weeks, a few minutes at a time of this daily activity will improve your equilibrium.

It's important that while you're doing this, you pay attention to each part of your body; notice the sensations of each muscle and joint and see how everything participates in this motion.

## Extricate Yourself – Be Still

It is possible to get *too* deeply into your head. If you find yourself beating your brains out against what feels like an immovable stone wall, it's time to extract yourself from your thoughts. We can become so determined to push through a problem one particular way that we forget there may be an easier solution to be found, simply by approaching it from a different direction.

When you find yourself brute-forcing your way forward, stop working, get up and step away, take a deep breath, and give your thoughts a chance to catch up with where you are. Stand, lie, or sit perfectly still.

Consciously relax first your shoulders, your upper arms, your lower arms, your wrists, and then each finger. Relax your legs the in same way, one muscle group at a time; then do the same with your head, neck, and torso. Either close your eyes completely or soften your gaze until you're not looking at anything specific

Remain as still as possible and let your brain wind down from its frenetic pace. If it's been a highly stimulating day, you may need to give your brain some time to simmer down before your thoughts will stop demanding your immediate attention.

When you've become completely quiet, remain still, open your inner ears, and listen. Listen to your gut instinct, to that still small voice; it may be trying to tell you something that will help you.

Then, when you're ready to move again, gradually transition to an upright posture and gently re-enter your work.

## Get Outside Of You

Songwriting is often a solitary activity, so it's important that you periodically take breaks that will reconnect you with both the physical world around you and with other people. Even the shyest individuals and the quietest loners need at least a *little* social interaction to maintain their physical, mental and emotional balance.

Here is a list of suggestions that vary in intensity, but will help you dig yourself out of whatever songwriting hole you've found yourself in. I suggest you choose a few that you like and mix them up a bit, every now and then, for variety.

- Go for a change of scenery. Many times, this will get your sense of adventure kicked into gear, so when you get back you can work effectively once more. Try going to the beach, a park, a river, or just imagine yourself where you want to be. Sometimes, simply moving your chair around or going to another room can help.

- It's often amazing how a simple shift in posture can make a huge difference. If you're sitting, stand up for a while. Walk around. Pacing can help, especially as you're developing your melodies.

- Play. Play with a dog, a cat, or with children. Let yourself be fully present in the moment, just as you are. Take your cues from them. Follow their lead.

- Phone a friend and just chat about anything *but* music for a few minutes.

- Run a short errand. Just remember to come back. Physically go into a place of business when it's open and interact with a live person instead of mailing, emailing, phoning, or dropping communications into a mail slot.

- Vacuum a floor. Wash a window, take out the trash, straighten your books, or do anything else that needs to be done. The physical movement alone can relax and jar loose the cogs in your mind, so that when you return to writing, you will approach your song from a fresh perspective.

You'll notice I said nothing about texting, checking Facebook, or connecting with any sort of social media applications. This is intentional. Your greatest need when you're stuck, is to *get away* from mental space, *not* to exchange one form of mental space for another. That's why I emphasize getting yourself into contact with the real world, tangible things that will help jog your whole self into connection with what lies outside of your head.

I have another reason for this; **the real world is where the ideas are hanging out**. That's where all your senses get revitalized with fresh sights, sounds, smells, sensations. Any interactions you engage in while on break have the potential for providing the seeds of future creativity. But these seeds will only be planted when you get outside of your head and reconnect with your physical, relational, and spiritual senses.

## Exercise: Free-flow

You can use this to warm up when you begin your writing sessions; you'll find it equally helpful for getting yourself unstuck. Set yourself to thinking up a melody; play with it and develop it in your head for three minutes.

Alternatively, pick up your main instrument and just play notes at random, shaping them melodically into whatever you want...for three minutes. Don't attempt to censor or mold your music into anything in particular; just open up a conduit from your mind straight to your instrument and let it all flow out.

## Remember Your Foundations

Keep in mind that the four foundational pillars of creativity are Gratitude, Exercise, Mindfulness and Sleep. Are any of these lacking in your life. Is there one activity can you start doing right now will have a significant impact on your motivation and productivity?

# Conclusion

You now have everything you need to successfully write all the songs inside of you. You have **a process** to follow as you craft your melodies. Any time you get stuck, you can return to the applicable chapter and practice any of the **targeted exercises** that fit your situation.

You also understand how to follow **musical arcs** in your songwriting. You are developing a feel for when a melodic line needs to rise and fall.

Finally, you know how to combine melodic and harmonic lines to generate the songs that your audience will flock to hear.

Moving forward, here's what I recommend:

- Continue to write. Keep on repeating this process until **you have written at least five songs**. Only then will you know enough to decide how far you want to take this dream of yours.

- Keep on writing. If you write by fits and starts, that's okay. <u>Just keep writing</u>.

- Remind yourself frequently that songwriting is more a *skill* than a *gift*; therefore, **it <u>can</u> be learned**.

- Sharpen your writing skills, using the provided practice exercises, to target each area of music writing. Repeat these exercises regularly, modifying them as needed to address specific weak areas in your writing.

- **Listen** to music. Lots of music, with an ear to discovering *how* and *why* successful songwriters did what they did. Borrow their tactics shamelessly; avoid violating their copy rights, but take their favorite compositional strategies and make them your own.

I hope you have enjoyed this book and will continue to use it as your **handbook for great songwriting** as you work toward mastering your expertise at music composition. I wish you the best.  Go ahead and take some action right now.  Choose the next song that is burning in your soul and take the first few steps to turn it into reality.

*Thank you* for reading this book.  I hope you are able to use it to **write many great songs.**  I wish you the best.  Remember, just be patient, smart, and persistent and over time there will be no doubt as to who the great songwriter is!

*Thanks for reading.*

If this book has helped you or someone you know then I invite you to **Leave a Nice Review Right Now**; it would be greatly appreciated!

## My Other Books

For more great books simply visit my author page or type my name into the Kindle Store search bar or the Books search bar: **Susan Hollister**

## Author Page

**USA**: https://www.amazon.com/author/susanhollister

**UK**: http://amzn.to/2qiEzA9

*Thanks and Enjoy!*

Made in United States
Troutdale, OR
12/09/2024

25858804R00066